Philip H. Bagenal

The Priest in Politics

Philip H. Bagenal

The Priest in Politics

ISBN/EAN: 9783337070274

Printed in Europe, USA, Canada, Australia, Japan

Cover: Foto ©Suzi / pixelio.de

More available books at **www.hansebooks.com**

THE PRIEST IN POLITICS.

BY

PHILIP H. BAGENAL,

AUTHOR OF
"THE AMERICAN IRISH AND THEIR INFLUENCE
ON IRISH POLITICS," ETC.

LONDON:
HUTCHINSON AND CO.,
34, PATERNOSTER ROW.
1893.

PREFACE.

THIS book has been called forth by the necessities of a great crisis. It seemed to me of the highest importance that some connected narrative should be given of the action of the Irish Roman Catholic priest in the political life of Ireland during recent years. I have been a student of Irish affairs for the past fifteen years, and I can claim to have intimate knowledge of Irish political history during that period. Part of the time I was engaged in conducting a weekly newspaper in Dublin, and the events which I relate, passing as they did before my very eyes, necessarily became deeply impressed upon my mind.

Viewed in its true perspective, who can say the political attitude to-day of the Irish Roman Catholic hierarchy is not fraught with tremendous consequences? The recent protest of an important section of the Roman Catholic community demonstrates that there is grave uneasiness in many minds outside the Protestant churches at the unparalleled position and conduct in politics of the Roman Catholic clergy.

My last desire has been to attack in any way the tenets or religious convictions of Roman Catholics, and I wish to deprecate in the strongest possible manner any idea that such is the aim or scope of this publication. My sole object has been to awaken men's minds in Great Britain to the actual facts of the situation, and to show what has been said and what has been done by Irish priests in Irish politics in recent years. I hardly think the Roman Catholic clergy themselves at all appreciate the trend and logical result of their own action. Perhaps when they see it in all its startling nakedness they may be awakened to a sense of the dangers which surround them.

On the other hand, I have endeavoured as strongly as I can to emphasise the existence of two distinct communities in Ireland, and to show the depth of the earnestness and determination which animate the Irish Protestants in their resistance to Home Rule. Their feelings and opinions may be right or wrong, but they exist largely, because of the action of the priest in politics, and it is right their attitude should be fully appreciated.

I acknowledge with pleasure my indebtedness in points of matter, phrase, expression and inspiration to many interesting books dealing with Irish affairs —more especially to Mr. Harrison's *The Scot in Ulster*, Mr. Goldwin Smith's *Canada and the Canadian Question*, and his *Irish History and Irish Character*; Mr. Nassau Senior's *Journals and Conversations in Ireland*; to *Pictures in Ireland*, by Terence McGrath; *Paddy at Home*, by Baron de Mandat-Grancy; last, but not least, to the Right Hon. W. E. Gladstone's pamphlets upon *Vaticanism* and *The Vatican Decrees*, and generally to the various publications of the Irish Unionist Alliance.

P. H. B.

48, Editii Road,
   West Kensington, W.

CONTENTS.

CHAPTER I.

INTRODUCTORY 1

CHAPTER II.

THE CHURCH OF ROME IN IRELAND.

Policy of the Roman Catholic Church under Cardinals Cullen and McCabe. Opposed to Revolutionary Movement. Change of front after the Death of Cardinal McCabe. The Policy of Archbishop Walsh. 4

CHAPTER III.

THE CLAIMS OF IRISH SACERDOTALISM.

The Case of Messrs. Cogan and Ryan. Extraordinary Claims of Archbishops Walsh and Croke. Cardinal Logue on Parnellism. The Plan of Campaign. Its Reception by Archbishops Walsh and Croke. The Cases of Father Keller and Father Ryan. 13

CHAPTER IV.

SOME CATHOLIC VIEWS OF IRISH PROTESTANTISM.

Mr. Biggar's Views. The *Irish World* on Irish Presbyterians. The Jesuits on Home Rule. Extraordinary Speech by Father Hughes. Scotch Children Boycotted. A Meath Priest on Protestantism. Mr. Healy on Catholic Claims. . . . 26

CHAPTER V.

POSITION OF THE IRISH PRIEST; HIS INFLUENCE, AND HOW HE USED IT.

Birth and Education of the Irish Priest. Early Impressions and Feelings. Exceptional Position. His Leadership in Local Politics. The National League Code enforced by Priests. Instances of Action of Priests in carrying out the Behests the League. 39

CHAPTER VI.

ACTION OF THE IRISH PRIESTS IN POLITICS.

Violent Language of an American Priest. Cases quoted in Special Commission. Imprisonment of Two Priests for Breaking the Law. Father McFadden. Intimidation by Priests in Local Elections. 54

CHAPTER VII.

THE PARNELL DIVORCE CASE—AND AFTER.

Sketch of the Episode. Attitude of the Irish Roman Catholic Hierarchy. Their Decision, when and how Given. The New Plan of Campaign. Mr. Leamy, M.P., on the Bishops' Views. 75

CHAPTER VIII.

THE PRIEST AT BYE-ELECTIONS, 1890-92.

The Kilkenny Election. The *Star's* Correspondent thereon. The North Sligo Election. The Carlow Election. Action of Bishop Lynch. Descriptions by Parnellite M.P.'s of the conduct of the Election. The Cork Election. Canon O'Mahony's Advice. The Waterford Election . . . 84

CHAPTER IX.

THE GENERAL ELECTION, 1892.

The Cork Election. Extraordinary Letters of Canon O'Mahony. Mr. W. Redmond's Correspondence with the Canon. Mr.

CONTENTS.   xi

PAGE

Corbet, M.P., on the Wicklow Election. The South Tipperary Election. Mr. J. O'Connor's Account. The North Galway Election. Priests Rioting. Archbishop Croke on Home Rule. 97

CHAPTER X.

THE SOUTH MEATH ELECTION, 1892.

A Clerical Caucus. The Campaign against Independent Political Opinion. The Bishop of Meath's Thunder. "The Shadow of Sin." "Fire to their Heels and Toes." A Group of Startling Utterances. A Scene at a Death-bed. How the Petition was Treated. Attachment of Father Fay. A Comparison with English Clergy. 112

CHAPTER XI.

THE NORTH MEATH ELECTION.

Mr. Davitt's Plan of Campaign. Bishop Nulty's Sermon. Father Duffy's Stick. Father Clarke knocks down an Old Man. A Priest assaults a Child. 121

CHAPTER XII.

MR. GLADSTONE ON PRIESTS IN POLITICS.

Mr. Gladstone's Pamphlets in 1874—"The Vatican Decrees" and "Vaticanism." His Views upon the Claims of the Papacy. Description and Characterisation of the Church of Rome. Definition of Independence in a State. . . . 139

CHAPTER XIII.

LESSONS OF HISTORY.

Ireland in 1642. Action of Rinuccini, the Papal Nuncio, in 1645. The Roman Catholic Parliament in Ireland of James II. . 150

CHAPTER XIV.

THE CANADIAN PRIEST IN POLITICS.

Sketch of the Priestly Authority in Quebec. The Incidence of Taxation. The Claim of Ecclesiastical Immunity. Decisions of the Courts of Law. A Canadian Priest on Lay Obedience. Parallel of Ireland. 161

CHAPTER XV.

THE ATTITUDE OF IRISH PROTESTANTISM.

Mr. Disraeli's Curious Prediction in 1869. What the Irish Protestants Fear, and Why. Views of the Various Protestant Churches. Rev. J. Parker's Admission. . . . 171

CHAPTER XVI.

THE SCOT IN ULSTER.

The First Scottish Colonies. The Great Plantation of Ulster. The Fortunes of the Colonists in the 17th and 18th centuries. Ulster since the Union. 182

CHAPTER XVII.

THE BELFAST CONVENTION.

The Scene at the Convention. Composition of the Demonstration. The Character of Ulstermen. Motive of the Meeting. Justification of the Union. Why and How Ulster will fight. The Resolutions arrived at. 193

CHAPTER XVIII.

SUMMARY OF CONCLUSIONS 208

THE PRIEST IN POLITICS.

CHAPTER I.

INTRODUCTORY.

"IT is the peculiarity of Roman theology," said Mr. Gladstone nineteen years ago, "that by thrusting itself into the temporal domain, it naturally, and even necessarily, comes to be a frequent theme of political discussion." The events of the past two years have confirmed the truth of the view expressed by the Prime Minister in 1874. But at the very outset it is most earnestly to be desired that all religious bigotry may be eschewed in the remarks now offered upon the present crisis in Imperial affairs. Facts hold the field—facts of current history and facts of belief, facts which must necessarily be taken into account in dealing with the present state of Ireland and the divided race which inhabits her shores. The split in the Nationalist party; the attitude thereon taken by the Roman Catholic hierarchy in regard to Irish politics, and its bearing upon the civil and religious liberties of mankind at large; the action of the Bishop of Meath and the priesthood of his diocese, and the judgments of the Courts established by Parliament to try election petitions—all these are subjects which go to the root of the problem of "the priest in politics," and as such demand plain and unsparing treatment at the hands of contemporary writers. It is absolutely necessary to ascertain the "climate of opinion" in Ireland at the present day, to trace its origin and its results, and to lay some conclusions before the jury of British public opinion before another verdict is taken upon the issue of Union or Separation.

Why is it that the Irish Nonconformists of all denominations have thrown off their old allegiance to the Liberal party ever since Mr. Gladstone adopted the Home Rule programme? Simply because they believe that under a Roman Catholic Parliament in Dublin civil and religious liberty would become a shadow instead of a reality. Why have the Irish Presbyterians and Methodists and Baptists and Congregationalists supported in every possible way Lord Salisbury's Government and a party which only a few years ago they invariably opposed? Because they are convinced by special local knowledge that their only guarantee against the undue ascendency in Church and State of the Roman Catholic hierarchy is the continued existence of an Imperial Parliament at Westminster. Rightly or wrongly, moreover, the whole Protestant community of Ireland, Episcopalian and Nonconformist, are strongly of opinion that in the event of the establishment of a Dublin Parliament the same influences which twelve years ago brought about revolutionary violence, chaos, and social disorder in Ireland would be set in motion to make the lot of Protestants, as a political community, insupportable.

I propose to give some of the facts on which these opinions are based. Protestant Ulster will never submit to be governed by a Roman Catholic Nationalist majority in Dublin. That is a fact which should be thoroughly understood. It is one of the characteristics of Mr. Gladstone's methods of getting up a political subject that he keeps in shadow all the adverse points, and slurs over the most important arguments against his own position.

It seems impossible for him either to believe or to realise what is the length and breadth and height of the Irish Protestant antagonism to Home Rule.

It is the object of these pages to lay before Mr. Gladstone's followers and the public generally the real nature of the present religious and political crisis, and how it is viewed by over a million and a half of Protestant Irish people who resent and are determined to struggle against, amongst other things, the attempt of priests to "trespass on ground which belongs to the civil authority, and to determine by spiritual prerogative questions of the civil sphere."*

---

* "The Vatican Decrees in their Bearing on Civil and Religious Liberty." By Right Hon. W. E. Gladstone, M.P J. Murray, London, 1874: pp. 9, 10.

CHAPTER II.

THE CHURCH OF ROME IN IRELAND

CHANGE IN THE POLICY OF THE ROMAN CATHOLIC CHURCH.

NOTHING is more striking than the complete change of front which has taken place amongst the representatives of the Church of Rome in Ireland during the last ten years. From 1853 to 1883 the efforts of the Church of Rome were undoubtedly directed towards suppressing secret societies, discouraging seditions, and checking all illegal agitation in Ireland. Cardinal Cullen and Cardinal M'Cabe broke down Ribbonism, opposed Fenianism and all revolutionary movements. Cardinal M'Cabe discerned very quickly the forces of violence which were behind Mr. Parnell, and denounced the Clan-na-Gael and the Irish-American policy of Mr. Davitt and the Land League. He openly opposed Mr. Parnell, and endeavoured to break his popularity and curb his power. The object of the Church of Rome in carrying out this policy was, no doubt, to keep in its hands without ostentation, and yet with a full consciousness of strength, political power at the polls, as well as moral suasion over the people.

It must, however, be said, in justice to such ecclesiastical statesmen as Cardinals Cullen and M'Cabe, that they had confidence in the justice of the men who were at the head of the State, and believed that Ireland could obtain what she wanted in the region of political reform much more safely and readily if only she adopted a course which the law allowed, and if she avoided giving cause of offence. No better proof of their wisdom could be given than the present disorganisation of political and religious thought in Ireland. The manifesto of the Unionist Roman Catholics of Ireland, put forth in March 1893, proves conclusively that there is still a large and influential section of the Irish population who hold to the older and wiser policy of the Church of Rome with regard to Irish political questions.

Archbishop Walsh's New Departure.

The success of Mr. Parnell in spite of the opposition of the Pope and of Cardinal M'Cabe led to a complete change of tactics on the part of the Roman Catholic hierarchy. On the death of Cardinal M'Cabe, in 1885, it was determined by Archbishops Walsh and Croke to capture the Nationalist movement, and by pretending to head it to regain the popularity which the late

* *Times*, March 15th, 1893.

Cardinal's action had so seriously jeopardised. For some years, indeed, as will be presently shown, the priesthood had given every possible assistance to the movement against British law, and particularly with regard to the land question. But the bishops had not fully and finally swallowed the principles of the New Ribbonism, or adopted blindly the leadership of Mr. Parnell. It was not until after Cardinal M'Cabe's death that there was practically a conspiracy set on foot between the Nationalist press and the Irish hierarchy to persuade the Pope to reverse the policy of the Cardinal, and to allow his representatives in Ireland to adopt altogether new means for regaining the leadership of Irish political opinion. It is well known that the Pope desired to appoint Dr. Moran, the Archbishop of Sydney, and now a Cardinal, to succeed Cardinal M'Cabe; but the pressure from Ireland was too strong, and Dr. Walsh was made Archbishop of Dublin. How far the new departure would have been successful had Mr. Parnell not fallen from his high estate, no one can now surmise. But recent events prove beyond dispute that when the opportunity of getting rid of so powerful a Protestant leader offered, it was taken and utilised by the Roman Catholic hierarchy in a manner which was quite unmistakable.

How, then, did the Irish hierarchy and priesthood set to work in 1885 ? They not only identified themselves more and more closely with the political action of the Nationalist party, but they embarked with a light heart in the social war which was then raging in Ireland. And this was done in the very teeth of definite commands to the contrary from the late ecclesiastical authority.

Broken Conditions.

In 1882, after the terrible tragedy in the Phœnix Park, Cardinal M'Cabe convened the hierarchy in solemn conclave in Dublin, and addressed a joint letter to the Irish people. In this document it was clearly laid down on what conditions the Irish clergy undertook to countenance the cause of Irish nationality. These conditions were that the five most common means of promoting Mr. Parnell's movement should be abandoned—viz. : (1) refusal to pay rent, (2) preventing others from paying rent, (3) boycotting and agrarian crime, (4) resisting bailiffs, (5) forming secret associations for the promotion of the above objects, or obeying the orders of such associations.

Ever since Archbishop Walsh assumed the reins of ecclesiastical government in Ireland, the priesthood have not only not observed the above conditions, but have supported the perpetration of these illegal deeds, and in many cases, as we shall presently show, committed them in person. The circular letter of 1882 denouncing these practices contained the following adjuration :—

" Under each of these offences we solemnly protest in the name of God and of His holy Church ; and we declare it to be your duty to regard as the worst enemy of your creed and country the man who would recommend or justify the commission of any of them." *

In spite of these injunctions and subsequently of the still more precise commandments of the Pope himself, the Irish priesthood were for years the head and front of every form of resistance to the law of the land.

Archbishop Walsh Repudiates Statute Law.

Amongst the Irish hierarchy none have been more outspoken in their sympathy with resistance to the authority of the State than Archbishop Walsh and Archbishop Croke, who preside respectively over the dioceses of Dublin and Cashel. Perhaps the most truculent remark which ever fell from a prelate's lips came from Archbishop Walsh in 1887. Referring to the Crimes Act, he said:—

"I can only say of it that whatever may be its technically binding force . . . it commands no more respect from me than if it had been forced through Parliament by means of a resolution passed by the majority of the House of Commons, withdrawing the Constitutional right of voting from every member of that House who did not happen to sit upon the Ministerial bench." †

---

* See my article in *Blackwood's Magazine*, June 1888, for text of this state paper and others mentioned in the course of this volume.

† *Freeman's Journal*, Nov. 25th, 1887.

Is it any wonder that the Irish peasantry are lawless, and that social order has barely survived, when the head of the Roman Catholic Church in Ireland could thus write to a public journal? Such is Dr. Walsh's idea of the subjection he owes to the law.

ARCHBISHOP CROKE'S POLITICAL RECORD.

But Archbishop Walsh has always been put in the shade by Archbishop Croke. This prelate admits the soft impeachment that when he was a young man, in 1848, he helped John Mitchell and James Fintan Lalor, two of the most violent patriots of that day, to broach the very same scheme of resistance to rent which was developed forty years after into the Plan of Campaign. Ever since the Land League movement commenced, in 1879, Archbishop Croke has aided and abetted the most violent sections of the Nationalist party. Mr. Parnell was his "white-haired boy." He it was who set on foot the national testimonial to the Irish leader in 1883. The movement was condemned by the Vatican, and Dr. Croke summoned for censure to Rome. Archbishop Croke helped to found the Gaelic Athletic Association, which was well known to be a physical-force movement in disguise. He subscribed in 1886 £5 to the Manchester Martyrs' Memorial Fund, and accompanied it with a letter declaring that the men who caused the death of Sergeant Brett were "wrongfully arrested, unfairly tried, and barbarously executed," and went like "heroes to their doom." With Fenianism the Archbishop has always had considerable sympathy, and he recently supported a movement to raise a fund to pension James Stephens, the old revolutionary Head-Centre of the Irish Republican Brotherhood.

Whitewashing the Plan of Campaign.

Both these prelates helped to launch the Plan of Campaign in 1886. Archbishop Walsh, interviewed by the *Pall Mall Gazette*, thus spoke of the system of "organised embezzlement" which was afterwards specifically condemned by the Court of Rome.

"I confess," he said, "that at first I was a little startled at it. I was not only startled, but grieved. But when I looked into the matter carefully, my anxiety was relieved. Of course, the great difficulty (indeed I may say the only one) was that the 'Plan of Campaign' leaves it practically to the judgment of the tenants, that is to say, to the judgment of one of the parties to the contract of tenancy, to fix the terms on which that contract is to continue in force. That, no doubt, in the abstract seems at first sight a formidable difficulty; but we must look at the other side of the question. If the tenant is to be viewed merely as one of the two parties to the rent contract, in what other light are we to view the landlord? He, too, is only one of the contracting parties, and he has had the fixing of the terms of the contract long enough.

It is quite clear that the tenants are not to be blamed if they claim to have their turn now."*

A more absurd attempt to whitewash the Plan of Campaign could not be imagined. Contracts depend upon agreement between the parties. The Campaigners used the land, kept the rent and possession of the land, and refused either land or a part of the produce as expressed in rent to the owner. And an archbishop of the Church of Rome declared under such circumstances he was quite clear that the tenant who adopted the Plan of Campaign was not to be blamed! The Pope took a different view. The Plan of Campaign was condemned by a special Court of Cardinals, and Archbishop Walsh's chance of the Red Hat was thereby lost for ever.

Pay no Taxes.

It is hardly necessary to say that Archbishop Croke decided to "go one better" than his brother in Dublin. The Government decided to test the legality of the Plan of Campaign in the courts of law, and a national subscription was immediately set on foot. Archbishop Croke subscribed both money and political advice. His letter on the subject was a nine days' wonder at the time.†

"I opposed," he said, "the No Rent Manifesto six years ago, partly because, apart from other reasons, I

---

* *Pall Mall Gazette*, Dec. 1st, 1886.
† *Freeman's Journal*, Feb. 18th, 1887.

thought it was inopportune and not likely to be acted on. Had a manifesto against paying taxes been issued at the time, I should certainly have supported it on principle."

No wonder Mr. Davitt called Dr. Croke's letter "priceless"! The fact that it could be written by a Roman Catholic prelate shows how easily a movement could be set on foot against the payment of a "contribution" to England under a Home Rule scheme which was not exactly drawn on the financial lines approved by the Nationalist party.

When priests commit and condone the offences which they are specially enjoined by their own highest ecclesiastical authority to denounce, then we may fairly say they are demoralised; we may spurn all paper guarantees against abuse of their spiritual and temporal powers; we may declare that it is impossible for civil and religious liberty to exist when they are clothed with authority over the lives and properties of their fellow-countrymen who differ from them in religious belief. Nay, more: it is lawful, and may be necessary, to oppose physical force to any attempt to place the neck of the Protestant community underneath the heel of an authority imbued with such curious ideas of the sanctity of the law.

CHAPTER III.

THE CLAIMS OF IRISH SACERDOTALISM

THE BOYCOTTING OF POLITICAL OPINION.

ARCHBISHOP WALSH was not long in giving the world a taste of his quality. The general election of 1885 gave him an opportunity which he quickly improved. In the course of the elections two Catholic laymen, the Right Honourable W. Cogan, formerly member for County Kildare, and Mr. George Ryan, of Inch—the latter a Loyalist candidate for Tipperary—ventured to criticise in severe terms the supporters of the National League. Mr. Cogan wrote a letter to the *Freeman's Journal*, in which, after alluding to the policy and principles of Archbishop Murray and Cardinals Cullen and M'Cabe, he said: "It is the duty of every man to come forward and take his side; it is the part of a coward to shirk it. One must be in favour of law and order and loyalty, and the continuance of the legislative Union of this country under the sovereignty of the Queen, or in favour of an illegal conspiracy against law and individual liberty."

To the ordinary British mind there is nothing particularly remarkable in such a summing-up of the political situation in 1885. But Archbishop Walsh thought otherwise. He replied in a letter to the public press in a manner which surprised even his own co-religionists. He declared that Mr. Cogan had publicly libelled him, and he complained that he had been criticised in a manner inconsistent with the respect due by a Catholic to his archiepiscopal office.

Insulting the Archiepiscopal Office.

It was thus clearly laid down by the head of the Roman Catholic Church in Ireland that to criticise the National League was not only to publicly insult Dr. Walsh personally as a politician and a supporter of the League, but also the archiepiscopal office itself! Could anything be more glaring than this assumption? Does it not declare that civil rights are not made for Catholic laymen? and is it not a distinct attempt upon the part of Archbishop Walsh to shelter himself behind his sacerdotal character from public criticism on public acts done in his political character? Such claims must, if admitted, place the clerical body in Ireland above criticism, and make the Catholic hierarchy the sole and despotic ruler of the people. They mean that when an archbishop holds certain political views all others who differ must keep silence. This is the boycotting of political opinion—nothing more and nothing less.

The infallibility of Archbishop Walsh in politics must be admitted on pain of archiepiscopal resentment.

POLITICAL CRITICISM INCONSISTENT WITH RESPECT TO THE CLERGY.

Archbishop Croke followed suit almost immediately. Mr. George Ryan did not even criticise or reply to an archbishop. He exercised his right of attacking Mr. Parnell's party, and sketched Mr. Parnell and his followers as "rogues" and "mendicant patriots" of the League, in a manner which was undoubtedly more vigorous than complimentary, but which has been quite equalled if not surpassed during the past two years by the rival factions of Nationalists in their abuse of one another. The reply came not from the politicians assailed, but from the Archbishop of the diocese. Dr. Croke wrote to the *Freeman's Journal* to lay down the principle that the criticism of a body of politicians "who are held in high repute by the overwhelming majority of the bishops and priests of Ireland" is inconsistent with the respect a Catholic layman owes to "the clergy generally, and the dignitaries of the Church." The monstrous doctrine, therefore, put forward by these two prelates was, and is, that when the clergy descend into the political arena they are not only entitled *ex officio* to exemption from the attacks to which all other politicians are exposed, but actually the whole party which at the time being they may patronise is to be hedged round with the reverence due to the Roman Catholic bishops and priests of Ireland.*

"No Dividing Line between Religion and Politics."

This doctrine is in full swing to-day in Ireland, as we shall see when we come to deal with the Meath election. Meanwhile, it should be noted that these views were never before put forward so boldly in Ireland until Archbishop Walsh came to the front. He has on several occasions, moreover, declared that it passes the wit of man to discover the dividing line between morals and politics. "In Ireland," he said, "the line between religion and politics is a line by no means easy to draw. I have some experience now in critically observing such matters, and I have never known that feat to be accomplished with perfect success." †

Two days afterwards Dr. Walsh claimed that the Roman Catholic clergy in Ireland possessed, "as priests, and independent of all human organisations, an inalienable and indisputable right to guide their people in this momentous proceeding, as in every other proceeding where the interests of Catholicity as well as the interests of Irish nationality are involved.‡

---

* For a full account of these extraordinary episodes see Mr. T. W. Rolleston's article in the February number of the *Dublin University Review*, 1886.

† *Freeman's Journal*, Sept. 18th, 1885.

‡ *Ibid*, Sept. 20th, 1885.

This attitude of omniscience and omnipotence taken up by the Church of Rome in Ireland with regard to politics was never so crudely laid before the country.

Ex-officio Clerical Franchise.

Even in the smallest details Archbishop Walsh was determined to carry out his policy. On September 4th, 1888, when he returned to Ireland from Rome, one of his first acts was to rescind the rule enforced by his predecessors, forbidding the clergy to take any part in any political demonstrations. That perhaps was a small matter. But the next step was a "bolt from the blue." He suggested, and the suggestion was adopted, that at all the political conventions held in the various Irish counties an ex-officio vote in the proceedings was given to the Roman Catholic clergy. This franchise could have had but one meaning. It embodied the principle in virtue of which, if Mr. Gladstone's Home Rule Bill became law, the priests of Ireland would become endowed with civil privileges which would make them *de facto* and *de jure* the absolute rulers of Ireland.

Cardinal Logue's View.

It may be said that Archbishop Walsh is discredited at Rome, and that these proceedings and utterances of his may be liberally discounted. But the new Irish cardinal, Archbishop Logue, of Armagh, has said substantially the same thing, and claims absolute obedience in political matters from the members of his Church.

"We are face to face," he said two years ago, "at the present moment with a great disobedience to ecclesiastical authority. The doctrines of the present day are calculated to wean the people from the priests' advice, to separate the priests from the people—to let the people use their own judgment. If that teaching goes on it will succeed in effecting what all the persecutions of England could never effect—it will succeed in destroying the faith of the Irish people.*

The disobedience alluded to was the refusal of Mr. Redmond's political party to desert the leadership of Mr. Parnell during his life, and after his death to obey the command of the Church with regard to their political conduct.

Canon Keller and Judge Boyd.

The claims of the hierarchy were fully supported by the priesthood. The Plan of Campaign was a political engine invented and set in motion by Messrs. Dillon and O'Brien in October 1886. The idea was an old one revived, the scheme being simply to use the resources of the landowner to fight a battle on the part of the tenant against paying rent, and thus to create a land war, which would force on a policy of coercion; this it was fully expected would divide the Unionists, and so make government in Ireland impossible. Mr.

* *National Press*, April 7th, 1891.

W. O'Brien, M.P., admitted in cross-examination in Cork, in 1888,* that he had got £4,000 in America to launch the social war. Mr. Harrington and other Parnellites have since admitted the whole thing was a political move. As we have seen, the Plan of Campaign was blessed by Archbishops Croke and Walsh at the outset. It was powerfully aided by the priests throughout the country. One of the earliest cases was the Ponsonby estate, in the county of Cork. The facts are clear. A tenant on the estate was adjudicated a bankrupt. Rev. Mr. Keller, the priest of Youghal, was summoned to give evidence in Dublin before Judge Boyd. He appeared in court accompanied by Archbishop Walsh, and was sworn. Being asked whether he remembered being in the Mall House, Youghal, on November 16th, 1886, he declined to answer, on the ground that he would not disclose any confidential statement made to him as a priest, and the drift of the question appeared to him to be to gain information of that kind. There was no suggestion in the case that Rev. Mr. Keller received information as to the whereabouts of the embezzled rent of the Ponsonby estate. He was a party to the breaking of the law, and his refusal to answer the question of the assignees in backruptcy was a direct contempt of Court. Rev. Mr. Keller was accordingly committed to jail. The scene on his removal is probably unparalleled. Seated in a cab, the recalcitrant priest, accompanied by Archbishop

* *Cork Constitution*, July 25th, 1888.

Walsh, was dragged by a vast mob to Kilmainham, the people shouting and singing, "We'll hang Judge Boyd on a sour apple tree."

Here we have the claim of the Roman Catholic priest stoutly made in a court of law that he is above the law, that it is his right and duty in civil cases to answer or not as pleases him. It is no longer limited to the secrets of the confessional. Like Rev. Mr. Keller, any priest may join a criminal conspiracy, may become the trustee of rents due to the landlord or any other creditor; but his honour as a priest forbids him to answer any question that might even tend to a disclosure of the truth! The discipline of the Roman Church is above the law of the land, and a priest's duty is relegated from a "higher source than the after-dinner wisdom of Westminster majorities."

Bishop M'Carthy Approves.

Rev. Mr. Keller's conduct was endorsed by his own bishop, Dr. M'Carthy, who wrote as follows: "As I am quite sure that you did nothing that you did not feel morally justified in doing, I am equally sure that any course you may adopt in consequence of it will be one that will meet with my approval." * Such a case as this roused the passions of the people to a terrible pitch. Cartoons were issued showing the prelates in vestments blessing the contumacious priest,

* *Freeman's Journal*, March 9th, 1887.

and the action of the Archbishop was quoted as proving the innocence of the priest and people.

The English Press took a very different view. Even the *Daily News* jibbed.

"Rev. Mr. Keller was summoned, not because he was a priest (an Irish judge would be mad who attempted to extract the secrets of the confessional), but because he is suspected of holding property belonging to the creditors of a bankrupt. He was committed for refusing to say whether he remembered being in the Mall House at Youghal on the 16th of November. It is quite obvious that the law of bankruptcy cannot be administered if a priest may take charge of a bankrupt's money, and may not be compelled to answer any questions about it. The prospects of Home Rule are excellent, and the Government is materially assisting them. Nothing can injure them, except the suspicion that English Home Rulers are favourable to anarchy."*

English Roman Catholics were scandalised at these proceedings of their Church in Ireland. Mr. de Lisle, who then sat for a division of Leicestershire, was very outspoken in his opinion. "I shall be told," he wrote, "that the new-born Celticism which defies the Queen's Law in Ireland has the blessing of two archbishops, half a hierarchy, a crowd of clergy, and some three millions of people, represented by eighty-five Nationalists in the Imperial Parliament. So much the worse

* *Daily News*, March 21st, 1887.

for them from the moral point of view, if in the pursuit of an object, even if in itself it be laudable, they transgress the ordinances of legitimate authority, where these ordinances are just and legal. The more sacred the office, the more scandalous the breach of the law."

In a letter to a Roman Catholic paper Mr. de Lisle also declared that "it is sedition to defy the law and to denounce legal obligation. Sedition may become sacrilegious. It cannot be sanctified."*

Father Ryan's Case.

Of course, Rev. Mr. Keller's example was immediately followed. A notorious priest, Rev. Matthew Ryan, of Hospital, County Limerick, surnamed "The General" in his district, from his warlike propensities, was summoned under similar circumstances to the Court of Bankruptcy, and refused to give any information regarding the disposal of the money of the Herbertstown tenantry. Speaking at a public meeting in Dublin before his appearance in court, he said :—

"The people among whom he lived called him 'The General,' but he was a general in command under the man who wielded the marshal's baton so ably and so skilfully—William O'Brien. His first duty was to thank them from his heart of hearts for the more than royal welcome they had given him that evening. He

* Article by Edward de Lisle, M.P., on "Shall England Rule?" *Union*, March 26th, 1887. See also his letter to the *Universe*, March 5th, 1887.

hoped to be in Kilmainham Prison to-morrow, and it had always been his hope to be allowed the honour of suffering in the cause of Irish nationality. He could assure them that Judge Boyd would not wring any evidence from him. He might be guilty of contempt of court if he declined to answer Judge Boyd to-morrow, but if he did answer he would be guilty of contempt of the Court of Heaven, and with these alternatives he need not tell them the one he would adopt. He would be guilty of contempt of Judge Boyd's Court. . . . He was consoled, comforted, and strengthened by the approbation of the great and good Archbishop of Dublin, and his own beloved Archbishop of Cashel, as well as of his own conscience. He was ready to speak, to do, to dare, and to suffer for the sacred cause of Ireland." *

The bellicose priest was as good as his word. He defied the law and refused to speak in the witness box as to his part in the Plan of Campaign. After his committal Rev. Mr. Ryan was driven to prison, while the Lord Mayor of Dublin and Archbishop Croke stood waving their hats and cheering amongst the mob. The National press, in commenting upon the case, declared that the priests of the Church were only vindicating ecclesiastical privilege. Archbishop Croke subsequently countenanced Rev. Mr. Ryan's escape from justice when the messenger of the Court of Bankruptcy came to seize him in his own parish on a second contempt of court.

* *Freeman's Journal*, March 29th, 1887.

On Sunday, May 29th, 1887, Rev. Mr. Ryan addressed a meeting at Herbertstown, when he gave utterance to the following political forecast: "The mettle of those around him would be put to a severe test in a few months. The Coercion Bill introduced by Balfour of the Long Legs would have passed into law unless the Great Campaigner in Heaven, who struck down the sub-sheriff with epilepsy at Bodyke the other day, would still the limbs and deprive the governors of the country of their power." *

Lord Selborne's Opinion.

These facts are forgotten now by the vast bulk of the people in England. But they made deep impression upon thinking men at the time. The claims of the Roman Catholic priesthood to dispense with, to supersede and to overrule the law of the land first, and then every other law or moral obligation when it may in the natural course of events be auxiliary to the law, came upon many statesmen with a shock of surprise. Lord Selborne is not a man of rash judgment or of hasty utterance, but he protested against these extraordinary claims with all the force at his command. "I am not sure," he said, " that such a pretension as this would have been made even in the days of those extravagant claims to exemption from civil jurisdiction which were advanced in the middle ages on behalf of clergymen

* *Cork Daily Herald*, May 31st, 1887.

accused of crimes and from which it took centuries to deliver our national jurisprudence." *

A hundred years ago Blackstone said that "however in times of ignorance and superstition that monster in true policy may for a while subsist, of a body of men residing in the bowels of a State, and yet independent of its laws, yet, when learning and rational religion have a little enlightened men's minds, society can no longer endure an absurdity so gross as must destroy its very fundamentals."

Nevertheless, at the close of the nineteenth century, a body of men was found eager and willing to claim the right to live in Ireland, and yet be independent of the laws passed by the Imperial Parliament. The Irish Protestants know these claims have been put forward, and will be put forward again when occasion offers. Can any one blame the Ulster Protestants for believing that Ireland, under a Home Rule Roman Catholic Parliament, would be a miniature Papal State? They know something by history and experience of the fires that lie slumbering beneath the ashes.

* See his article in the *Liberal Unionist*, April 16th, 1887.

CHAPTER IV.

SOME CATHOLIC VIEWS OF IRISH PROTESTANTISM

IT is almost unnecessary to say what Irish Protestants have done for the empire. Derry walls attest the strength of the conviction which animated the hearts and minds of their forefathers; and the trumpet note of the Belfast Convention on the eve of the General Election of 1892, repeated in the manifesto of the Ulster Defence Union in 1893, proves that the same spirit lives and glows as ardently as ever in the men of the North of Ireland at the present day. What we desire rather to show is the feelings and sentiments which are entertained against Irish Protestantism by a section at least of the Church of Rome in Ireland, as expressed by some of those entitled to speak for it. We do this not for the purpose of perpetuating religious rancour. There are hundreds of thousands of Irish and English Roman Catholics as loyal to the Crown to-day as Lord Howard of Effingham was loyal to Queen Elizabeth when he led her fleets against the Spanish Armada. Irish Protestants do not pretend to have any monopoly of loyalty, and the views now to be quoted are given merely to show why Irish Protestants are alarmed at the trend of political events in Ireland.

Mr. Biggar's Views.

Mr. Biggar, M.P., at the very commencement of the Land League movement, 1879, gave his views of Irish Protestants. Speaking in Bermondsey on the "Future of the Irish Race," he said: "By the 'Irish race' he meant to include all Irishmen of the Roman Catholic faith, wherever they were to be found. Protestants he did not consider Irishmen at all. They were merely West Britons, who had been by accident born in Ireland, and from his own experience he could say they were the bitterest enemies of Ireland." *

It is hardly likely that such a speech would ever be forgotten by Irish Protestants, and the bare memory of it is quite enough to make Ulster laugh at the idea of any paper guarantees for civil and religious liberty and equality under Home Rule.

Again, there are over 600,000 Presbyterians in Ireland, and their congregations, numbering 359, adopted resolutions in 1886 denouncing the project of establishing Home Rule in their country. Whereupon the organ of the Irish in America declares—"The assumption that these people are Irish is preposterous. They are not Irish. Their fathers went to Ireland to plunder and exterminate the native race, and they

* *Times*, March 4th, 1879.

inherit and retain the spirit of their fathers. They are an alien element in the Irish population, and their resolutions against Home Rule are of no more account than similar resolutions passed in Scotland or England." *

Here, then, we have in 1886 the same view laid down by the Queen's Irish enemies in America as Mr. Biggar when a member of Parliament maintained on an English platform in the heart of London.

The people of Ulster believe that the object of a large section of the Nationalist Party is to replace an extinct Protestant ascendency by a new Roman Catholic ascendency, engineered by the Roman Catholic bishops and priests in an Irish Parliament manned by the nominees of the hierarchy of the Church of Rome.

This view may be wrong, but it is founded on facts established and sentiments expressed, which cannot be denied and ought not to be blinked. In 1891 the population of Ireland was 4,700,000. Of this number, the census returns show that some 3,500,000 are Roman Catholics, and from these the bulk of the Home Rule party is recruited. Mr. Biggar, as we see, in 1879 denied even the name of Irishmen to the minority of 1,200,000 Protestants.

"Contemptible Dastards."

The same sentiment was almost as nakedly avowed in 1888 by a Roman Catholic priest from a public

* *Irish World*, Feb. 27th, 1886.

platform in County Kildare. Speaking at Monastercvan in that year, the Rev. Mr. Hughes said : " But though 'All's well' is the defiant cry that rings along our line of battle, still we all feel that the strain is very severe, and that now, in the last hours of the struggle that has been going on for seven centuries, Ireland needs the helping hand of all her children. Now, that help Ireland does not receive from her Protestant children. (A voice—They are only stepchildren.) Where are the Protestant farmers of this parish ? Are they here to-day, as they ought to be ? No, they are not. I have just been informed that there are three or four present. I am very glad ; but, taking them as a body, we have a right to complain of their base conduct. I can admire consistency in any man. If these farmers showed a hatred for all the works and pomps of the National League, I could understand it ; but these Protestant fellow-countrymen of ours, who do not stir a hand or contribute a penny in sustainment of the land war, are amongst the first to enjoy the spoils of the victory we win. I say they are *contemptible dastards* ! (Cheers.) I say they are imbeciles, if they hope that by-and-by, when the fight is over and the battle won, their refusal to help us shall not be remembered. (Hear, hear, and cheers.) Let no man dare to say that this is bigotry."*

What, then, is bigotry? The Rev. Mr. Hughes endeavoured, in the latter portion of his speech, to

* *Leinster Leader*, Dec. 15th, 1888.

minimise his first statement by mentioning the names of Protestants who had been Nationalists. He might as well have contended that because Mr. Bradlaugh was an Atheist, therefore Englishmen as a body endorsed his views of religion. In this case the Protestant farmers of the district were few and far between, and the object and effect of this priest's speech were to intimidate and force them into the ranks of a Nationalist organisation. Bigotry is the boycotting of opinion; and that was the aim of the Rev. Father Hughes's speech.

A New View of Protestantism.

Just before Mr. Gladstone openly declared his adoption of Home Rule, at that time the leading organ of Catholicity and Home Rule in Ireland gave vent to the following views about Protestant England:—

"We contend that the good government of Ireland by England is impossible, not so much by reason of natural obstacles, but because of the radical, essential difference in the public order of the two countries. This, considered in the abstract, makes a gulf profound, impassable—an obstacle no human ingenuity can remove or overcome. It is that the one people is Christian and the other non-Christian. . . . To put the contrast again in the plainest form—the one order of civilisation is Christian, the other non-Christian; the one people has not only accepted, but retained with inviolable constancy the Christian faith; the other has not only rejected it, but has been for three centuries the leader of the great apostasy, and is at this day the principal obstacle to the conversion of the world."*

In this marvellous expression of Roman Catholic public opinion in Ireland, it should be particularly noted that even the name of Christians is denied to Protestants. How, then, would they be treated under a Home Rule Government? Might it not be said that if the sentiment expressed by the organ of the Roman Catholic Church in Ireland were accepted, the logical conclusion must be persecution? The principal "obstacle" to Roman Catholic ascendency in three provinces of Ireland would be Protestantism. *Ergo*, drive the "contemptible dastards," the "West Britons," the "alien element," right out. In Ulster, no doubt, where the Protestants are well able and ready to take care of themselves, the spirit of religious persecution, latent or patent, would be powerless. But how about the sequestered Protestants in the rest of Ireland? Their position under Home Rule would be intolerable, exposed to the malignity and the predatory instincts of their ancient foes. Nothing but the ægis of an Imperial Parliament could protect themselves and their property from the attacks of an Irish Parliament.

Boycotting Scotch Children.

Here again facts confront the Northern Protestants.

* *Freeman's Journal*, Feb. 18th, 1886.

Two instances may be given. In 1888, the children who attended Barrowhouse National School, near Athy, County Kildare, declared that they would not associate with the children of a Scotch Presbyterian caretaker who lived close by on a farm from which the tenant was evicted. This tenant had joined the Plan of Campaign, and had held the land for three years without paying any rent. He was then evicted. The children, no doubt, were egged on by their parents to desert the school: in any case, Lord Lansdowne's agent, Mr. J. T. Trench, received the following remarkable letter from the Roman Catholic priest of Athy upon the subject:—

"ATHY, *December 28th*, 1888.

"SIR,—I wish to bring under your notice a difficulty which has recently arisen at Barrowhouse, and which you alone can remedy. A caretaker living in Mr. D. Whelan's house has two boys whom he sends to the school there at the chapel. Their presence dispersed the other children, who will not associate with the strangers. The result is that the school is broken up. If I may suggest a remedy for this disorder, it is to ask you to order these children to come into the Model school at Athy, where they will meet their own co-religionists, the Scotch. It is not too far—three miles. Otherwise the school must be abolished altogether, and the disorder spread and perpetuated. This is more simple and reasonable than to ask you to withdraw those Scotch boys. For the interests of peace and harmony I ask you to interfere in this urgent case, and am,

"JAMES DOYLE, P.P.

"J. T. TRENCH."

This letter ought to open the eyes of the blindest partisan to the demoralisation of the Irish priesthood.

The National system of education in Ireland is to throw the schools equally open to all. The priest for political purposes proposed to teach the children to set at defiance the rules of the National Education Board, and to allow them to assume the government of the school. He, in fact, proposed to allow the children to decide who should attend the school, and asked Mr. Trench to co-operate with him in abandoning his authority as a man and a priest, and in giving a marked sanction to the principle of boycotting. The suggestion in the Rev. Mr. Doyle's letter should be noted that the reasons for the objections to the children were—(1) that they were strangers, (2) that they were Presbyterians, and (3) that they were Scotch. These sentiments are sufficient in themselves to account for the rooted distrust of the Ulster population, which is largely of Scotch origin, to any system of Home Rule. Can any one doubt that with a Roman Catholic Parliament dominant in Ireland the priesthood would have it in their power to impose conditions of education to the parents of Irish Protestants outside Ulster? This, at all events, is the firm conviction of

Irish Loyalists, and it is worthy of consideration by British Nonconformists.

"What is Pure Protestantism?"

But it may be asked, What do the priests in Ireland fear in Protestantism? Why are they likely, when they have the power, to boycott Protestants and Protestant opinion in the provinces where Roman Catholics are in the majority? The answer is to be found written with a bold hand in the evidence given in the South Meath election. The same reason which has impelled the Roman Catholic bishop and priesthood of the diocese of Meath to boycott the opinions of Mr. Redmond and his party will impel them to boycott Protestants when their views or their actions become obnoxious to them. And that reason is the claim advanced by Protestant laymen to exercise the right of private judgment. Michael Brien, a South Meath voter, swore that he heard Rev. Mr. Buchanan preach a sermon in Dangan Church on the Sunday before the South Meath election. He spoke from the altar, and read the following extract from the Parnellite newspaper, the Dublin *Independent*:—" Any man voting at an election should vote according to his own conscience, no matter what Dr. Nulty (or it might be any bishop) might say." Then Rev. Mr. Buchanan said "that this is pure Protestantism; now, that is Protestantism pure and simple." Rev. Mr. Buchanan was cross-examined upon this point, and his evidence is worthy of notice :—

"'You said that was preaching the doctrine of private judgment?' 'Yes.'

"'And you said that was pure Protestantism?' 'I may have used those words.'

"'That is to say, you won't contradict the witness who swears you did?' 'I will not.'

"Witness—'I didn't say that Parnellism was "pure Protestantism."'

"'That for the Parnellites to vote was "pure Protestantism." Is not that the sum and substance of it?' 'No; I was referring to the teaching in the *Independent* paper. I said when I read that that it was the Protestant doctrine of pure private judgment—that is, to act on a false conscience, and not to follow or inquire into the teachings of the bishops and priests.'

"'Would you mean a false conscience was this—to inquire into the teachings of the bishops and priests, and if a man agreed with them, then he had a right conscience, and if he disagreed, he had a false conscience?' 'No.'

"'What do you mean by a false conscience?' No answer."*

Here is the condemnation of the right of private judgment as exercised by Protestants in political

---

* "The South Meath Election." Verbatim Report. Published by the *Irish Independent* Printing Co., Ltd., College Green, Dublin, 1892. 8vo., 284 pages.

questions. Their conscience is termed false and their action must necessarily be denounced as contrary to faith and morals. These are the facts and opinions which have been startling more and more the feelings of Irish Protestants. Nor is there any withdrawal by the Irish hierarchy of their claims.

The Claims of the Church of Rome Defined by Mr. Healy.

The claim of the Roman Catholic Church in Ireland to make every political question one of morals was expressly urged and reiterated by Mr. Healy, M.P., as counsel for Mr. Fulham. These are his words:—

"His learned friends might not like the Roman Catholic doctrine,—the State might not like the Roman Catholic doctrine; but the Roman Catholic doctrine would not be changed for them. The rude peasants at Clonard gates said, 'If you want private judgment go to Roper.'* But for those who held with the doctrines of an Infallible Church, for those who held with Episcopacy descendant and traced from the apostles, for those who held that into almost all the relations of life questions of morality thrust themselves at every chink and cranny,—for such persons that Church, when such questions arose, would declare and would pronounce upon them. They might view with jealousy the concerted action of an organised priesthood, and

* Mr. Roper was the Protestant rector of a parish in South Meath.

enact laws to punish that priesthood; they might view with horror the doctrine which imported a binding sanction on the minds of the people to listen to the teaching of the pastorate. Let them root out that Church; they had the power. But so long as the State sanctioned toleration, so long as it was indifferent to the doctrine that was preached, so long the question of the truth or the untruth of that doctrine would not be questioned in a court of law, but so far as the Roman Catholic Church was concerned it would be a question for the Court of Rome."

Causes of Protestant Disquietude.

With such claims openly made and avowed in a court of law, it is not surprising that the Protestants look forward with dread to the time when the State will be in the hands of a body of men who, either directly or indirectly, can command the decision of an Irish Parliament. Mr. Davitt in an interview with the *Pall Mall Gazette* on May 12th, 1885, when asked how he proposed to deal with the question of Ulster:— " Leave them alone to us," he said, " and we will make short work of these gentry. They are not Irish; they are only English and Scotch who are settled among us; and it is preposterous that they should be allowed to dictate to Irishmen how Ireland should be governed."

The question of education, of the subsidising of the priesthood, of the resumption of churches—all these questions have only to be declared questions of morality, and the Church of Rome in Ireland would have the power and the will to "pronounce upon them." The *Irish Catholic's* comment upon the judgment in the South Meath case is full of significance:—

"Mr. Justice O'Brien's decision may have been as creditable to him as a lawyer as it was, in the tone and matter of many of its passages, discreditable to him as a Roman Catholic; but we have no hesitation in saying that if those at whose demand it was pronounced fancy that it will act as any deterrent to Irish priests from discharging their duties as electors and as citizens, as well as the friends and advisers of their people, they forget the courage, the constancy, and the patriotism of the unconquerable and devoted clergy of Ireland." *

When the Church of Rome has the power the hierarchy seek under Home Rule it will practically include the appointment of the judiciary. With Mr. Healy on the bench, there would be no fear of any judgments impugning the claims of the Irish hierarchy.

* *Irish Catholic*, Dec. 10th, 1892.

CHAPTER V.

POSITION OF THE IRISH PRIEST

WHAT part did the priests play in the terrible social war which raged in Ireland from 1879 to 1882, and also in the later years of the National League? The answer is writ large in the newspaper press of the period. Not only did they neglect their duty in the making of peace amongst their flock, but they became active agitators, often fierce political firebrands, rousing the worst passions of ignorant, and often superstitious, people, and leading them on to action which was subsequently condemned by a tribunal of British judges as contrary to law, and by the Pope himself as subversive of morality.

To make intelligible the whole influence of the Irish priest, direct and indirect, it is necessary here to give some brief account of his condition and the circumstances of his life and education. Unless his peculiar position is understood and appreciated it is impossible to realise the power he wields in Irish society. In the first place, as a rule, he is in full sympathy with the narrow, limited ideas, impressions, and tastes that surround him. In France a young peasant who has become a priest is no longer a peasant. His nature has been transformed during the years he has passed at college. He returns to his cure of souls a new being salaried by the State, and a public official. In Ireland a young curate or even a parish priest (nearly always the son of a small farmer) differs very little from his neighbour and former comrades.

Education and Breeding.

As a boy he had drunk in at his father's hearth the stories of the penal laws, and had heard the burden of Ireland's wrongs and woes reiterated year in and year out until it had become part of his being. Any literature that he had absorbed would have been a one-sided history of Ireland and the poetry of the days of '98 and '48. Then, entering Maynooth College, he found himself amongst a throng of students of his own class, all leavened with the same prejudices and conversing and thinking from the same point of view. What wonder, then, that on returning to take up his duties as a priest he was ready to engage with ardour in the political struggles of the time? The principal educators in Ireland have been the priests; their influence, and the direction in which it is exercised, depend largely on their intellectual and moral cultivation, and still more on the relation in which the priest stands to his flock. When he belongs to the mass of the people by birth; when his only experience of life has been the cabin, the village school, the ecclesiastical seminary and the parochial cure; when he is dependent on his flock for society, sympathy, and income, he is not likely to teach any opinions except those which his flock approve.

Unacquainted with men outside his own narrow range, in all probability profoundly ignorant of the political systems of the world, unable and unwilling to conceive the true relation of Ireland to the Empire, and ravished with the sounding phrases of patriotic demagogues, the young priest is bound, if for no other reason, by the force of his birth, breeding, and education, to swim with the stream, and if possible to keep ahead of the current.

Exceptional Condition of Ireland.

But there are other potent reasons why the Irish priest should adopt the popular cause. There is practically no middle class in Ireland. The priest, therefore, finds himself in a position to direct the social and political movement of his district, and has done so without a rival until the appearance of Mr. Parnell and that class of Irish-American agitators and journalists who have of late become so troublesome to the Church of Rome. The situation, therefore, in Ireland until very recently has been quite exceptional. No other country in the world furnishes the same social conditions which render the position of the priest in temporal affairs so unapproachably powerful. The only vulnerable point is his entire dependence upon the people for his maintenance.

Payment of Priests.

A clergy maintained on the voluntary principle is exposed to the temptation of preaching doctrines palatable to the prejudices and passions of their congregations. They are tempted to take a strong part in local politics for the purpose of maintaining their local influence. They are induced to wield their ecclesiastical authority to enforce the payment of contributions. The Irish priest lives by magnifying his office, by representing himself as holding the keys of salvation, and by making salvation depend on the work and observances which give him power and profit. The stipends of the Roman Catholic clergy are entirely dependent on the congregations. Two collections are made every year, and their income is further supplemented by fees on births, deaths, marriages, and other offerings of a freewill character. A parish priest usually receives from £250 to £400 a year, a curate £120 to £160. Hence his sentiments, education, and parentage all jump with his material interests, and there have not been wanting signs of late years that unless the priest in Ireland "goes with the people" he will suffer in purse as well as in reputation.

Threats to Withhold Dues.

The following is an example :—

"Ballylaneen Branch,
"*January* 30*th*, 1887.

" Mr. R. A. Power presided.

" Mr. Power proposed the following resolution :—

" Resolved—' That, as Catholics are bound by command to pay dues to their pastors towards their support and maintenance, the members of the Ballylaneen branch of the Irish National League are of opinion that Catholics are not bound by commandment to pay dues to priests to aid and assist grabbers to oppress the evicted poor. And, whereas the Rev. ——, and the Rev. ——, were known to inspect Mrs. Walshe's evicted farm at Carrigcastle, and aid the now notorious grabber (the brother of one Michael Walsh) in taking same,—we, the members of the Ballylaneen branch of the Irish National League, are of opinion that the parishioners of whatever parishes in the dioceses of Waterford and Lismore, in which the above-named priests are located, are not bound by the commandments of their Church until Michael Walsh gives back possession of the evicted farm of Mrs. Walsh at Carrigcastle, and that copies of this resolution be printed and forwarded to the different branches of the League in the dioceses of Waterford and Lismore, the unions of Kilmacthomas, Waterford, Lismore, and Carrick-on-Suir, for adoption.'

"Mr. Jeffry Sullivan, P.L.G., seconded the resolution, which was passed with acclamation."*

The Power of the Confessional.

Such, then, is the Irish priest. But, above and beyond all, he holds the power of the confessional-box. All the thoughts and acts of his congregation are known to him, and in his mind are all the secrets of the people. Absolutely obliterated is the secrecy of the ballot by the operation of the confessional. Unapproached in authority, he uses it without stint. The theory of his Church is based upon an attitude of submission to the ecclesiastical powers claiming to rule by Divine power, and nine-tenths of the Roman Catholic population yield that submission gladly and as of right. Some idea can now be formed of the force which such a man represents in every Irish parish. His word is accepted in lay matters as well as in spiritual. His example is followed eagerly, and where he goes the people follow, assured of comfort and support in this world and forgiveness in the next. Let us see how the Irish priesthood used this tremendous influence during the crisis of Ireland's latest revolution.

The Priests and the Land League.

If there is one fact more thoroughly established than another in the history of the Irish Nationalist organisations of the past fourteen years, it is that coercion

* *Munster Express*, Feb. 5th, 1887.

was daily exercised on the peaceable and law-abiding inhabitants of Ireland by means of outrages, intimidation, and boycotting. To this system of organised tyranny Roman Catholic priests not only gave the weight of their countenance, but too often of their active sympathy and co-operation. Mr. Gladstone, in his speech in the House of Commons, May 24th, 1882, thus described boycotting:—

"What is meant," said he, "by boycotting? In the first place, it is combined intimidation. In the second place, it is combined intimidation made use of for the purpose of destroying the private liberties of choice by fear of ruin and starvation. In the third place, that being what 'boycotting' is in itself, we must look to this: that the creed of 'boycotting,' like every other creed, requires a sanction, and that the sanction of 'boycotting'—that which stands in the rear of 'boycotting,' and by which alone 'boycotting' can in the long run be made thoroughly effective—is the murder which is not to be denounced."

The Penal Code Enforced by the Priest.

Sir Edward Clarke once hit the nail on the head when he described boycotting as "the application of a name which was not Christian to a practice which is not a Christian practice." Strange it is that in Ireland, the island of saints, this unchristian practice was largely carried on by Christian clergymen. The penal code of the Land League and of its successor, the National

League, was framed exactly on the lines of the penal code of Ribbonism, and the sanctions were the same. One of the most extraordinary revelations of modern history is that practically the very same system of agrarian terrorism and outrage which, when secretly organised and carried out by small groups of Irishmen up to 1879, was bitterly denounced and opposed by the Roman Catholic clergy, was encouraged and patronised by many of them when it came into the open light of day, and was developed and headed by Mr. Parnell, Mr. Davitt, and the rest of the Irish parliamentary party.

There is hardly an item in the whole penal codes of the Leagues which has not been supported on public platforms or deliberated upon with a view to punishment in private meetings by Irish priests. The offences to which the coercion of outrage, boycotting, and intimidation applied were as follows :—

1, Caretaking; 2, Herding; 3, Being unpopular as a landlord; 4, Acting as an agent; 5, Associating with boycotted persons; 6, Supplying the police when on unpopular duty; 7, Accommodating obnoxious persons; 8, Not joining the National League; 9, Being related to a boycotted person; 10, Having given evidence in a case of prosecution; 11, Driving the police in the execution of their duty; 12, Not voting for Nationalist candidates at Poor-law Guardian elections; 13, Being appointed teacher of a National School contrary to the wishes of the people; 14, Having caused a wife to change her religion; 15, Being suspected of having paid rent; 16, Not paying rent to local trustees; and 17, Having obtained compensation for having been shot at.

The New Inquisition.

The National League spread a network of branches all over the country, and in a vast number of cases the president was the Roman Catholic priest or curate. In 1886 the Cowper Commission presented to Parliament evidence and a report, which contains a mine of information upon the methods and practices of the priest in politics. The whole social and political life of the country was at that time, and until Mr. Balfour assumed office, under the thumb of the League, which, in its turn, was in almost every village aided and abetted by the ecclesiastical power. The unwritten law of the League was for the time as supreme in Ireland as though a Nationalist Parliament existed in Dublin. The village tribunals met regularly, and decided the conditions of life for all classes of men in the district. The chair was taken by the priest; men were summoned to appear before him to give account of their works. Condemned in their absence, his presence and action gave a religious sanction to his ukases. The best way to bring home the working of Home Rule under the National League, and the part played by the priest in Irish politics, is to give illustrations of cases where the priests presided at League committees and carried out the *lex loci*.

The perusal of the following group of cases, fully verified all, taken from the Irish press, gives an insight into the working of the political and revolutionary work which the Irish priests helped to do even so recently as 1887. In each case the priest presided over a political meeting, gave his sanction to sentiments of the organisation, and joined in the crusade against the civil liberties of his fellow-subjects.

"Mark Him Well."

Mullinavat Branch, Jan. 9th, 1887 : Rev. P. Meaney, C.C., in the chair :—

"We request that those who have not as yet paid in the subscriptions will do so immediately, thereby becoming members. He who has said, 'He who is not with Me is against Me,' cannot err. Applying this test to our organisation, we are forced to believe that every man who stands aloof, and assists not morally and materially the National League, is an enemy of that association. Go, mark him well. By the first of next month a list of the members will be published, for the information of every person interested. If it be not too much we invite the attention of merchants and shopkeepers generally to the list."—*Munster Express*, Jan. 15th, 1887.

"Miserable Individuals."

Tulla, Sunday, Feb. 20th: Rev. Mr. Quinn, and subsequently Mr. W. Molony, presided.

"The reverend president addressed the meeting on the necessity of a strict observance of the rules and resolutions of the organisation, and scathingly denounced the conduct of several miserable individuals who are constantly infringing on them. Rev. Mr. Quinn put it to the Committee if they would in future receive lying excuses from such persons; and the Committee most emphatically asserted that no excuses would in future be taken, and the members of the organisation were called on to show those persons how deeply their conduct is felt, by leaving men to enjoy life in a world of their own."—*Clare Examiner*, March 5th, 1887.

A Vote of Censure.

Moynalty and Newcastle: Rev. P. Gallagher, president, in the chair:—

"A vote of censure was passed on a family named Gearty for their scandalous intercourse with a local emergency man."—*United Ireland*, Feb. 12th, 1887.

Warning to Those not in Sympathy.

Gurteen, Sunday, Feb. 27th, 1887: the Very Rev. Canon O'Donohoe, president, in the chair:—

"Resolved that a collection for the defence of Messrs. Dillon and O'Brien be made during the ensuing week in this locality, and that not less than sixpence be accepted from any person. Any one not subscribing will be considered not in sympathy with the branch."—*Sligo Champion*, March 5th, 1887.

Apology and Absolution.

Ballyadams and Wolfhill, Jan. 30th, 1887: Rev. Maher, vice-president, presided:—

" E. Bulger, who was employed as Trenelis's housekeeper, came forward to announce that she had given up the position, and said she wished to apologise to the committee for not doing so sooner. She was taken in, inasmuch as she was unaware that the parties lately come were emergency men. Chairman: 'It affords me no pleasure to have to condemn any one. I have to act according to principle, irrespective of persons; but I will add that it now affords me the greatest possible pleasure to receive you back again, and to hear you say you were mistaken; and the committee, I am sure, are equally pleased.'"

Posting Names.

Kilshelan Branch, Feb. 13th, 1887: Rev. P. Dunphy, C.C., in the chair:—

"That all members who have not yet paid their subscriptions on or before the next meeting, which will be held on the last Sunday of this month, their names will be published and posted on the chapel gate for two consecutive Sundays."—*Munster Express*, Feb. 19th, 1887.

No Supplies to the Police.

Miltown-Malbay, Sunday, March 13th, 1887: Rev. P. White, P.P., in the chair:—

"That from this day forward, any person who supplies the police, while engaged in work which is opposed to the wishes of the people, with drink, food, or cars, be censured by this branch, and that no intercourse be held with them."—*United Ireland*, March 19th, 1887.

"Blacklegs to the Cause."

Bohola Mayo: Rev. John O'Grady, P.P., in the chair:—

"That any member who buys or sells to any grabber, or to any persons who assist at evictions, be expelled from this branch, and his name be published as a blackleg to the cause."—*United Ireland*, Feb. 12th, 1887.

Hunting to be Stopped.

Aghaboe Branch, Feb. 13th, 1887: Rev. T. J. Phelan, C.C., vice-president, presided:—

"That any master of hounds allowing obnoxious parties to hunt with him, and who, on receiving notification of same, fails to have those parties removed from the hunting-field, be no longer himself permitted to hunt."—*Leinster Leader*, Saturday, Feb. 19th, 1887.

Denouncing a Bank.

Shelburne (Tenants' Defence Association), March 13th, 1887: Rev. Canon Doyle, P.P., presiding:—

Proposed by P. Clery, P.L.G., seconded by M. Furlong:—

"That as the National Bank—the bank of the people—has refused to accommodate the oppressors of the poor evicted victims of landlord cruelty—viz., the emergency vice-guardians—we call upon the friends of the people to give their custom to that bank, and when the Bank of Ireland paper is offered them to demand gold. The Bank of Ireland has ranged itself in the ranks of our enemies."—*Wexford People*, March 19th, 1887.

A LIST OF PROSCRIBED NAMES.

Causeway Branch. A large meeting of this branch was held on Sunday last, Jan. 30th, 1887: Rev. T. Enright, P.P., president, in the chair:—

"The farmers of two neighbouring estates came before the meeting to consider the rent they could pay in those trying and depressed times. The conduct of several members, who had not renewed their subscriptions for last year, was strongly condemned, the reverend president giving orders to have a list, with their names, sent to him before the next meeting."—*Kerry Sentinel*, Feb. 4th, 1887.

BOYCOTTING THE PURCHASE OF LAND.

Mullahoran, Sunday, March 6th, 1887: Rev. J. Corcoran, P.P., in the chair:—

"After some routine business, a body of tenant

farmers were admitted, whose landlord offered to sell, and who came to ask the advice of the chairman on the subject of purchase. The reverend chairman gave a practical instruction on this subject, dwelling on the certain ruin of farmers who will buy on the landlord's present demands of seventeen and eighteen years' purchase, and advising the greatest caution in buying at all under present circumstances."—*Anglo-Celt*, March 12th, 1887.

Here we have the system which was denounced by the Pope in 1885, and subsequently in 1888, in full working order. The chapel doors are used as the sounding-boards of boycotting. The priest insists on the necessity of breaking the law, and sits in judgment to condemn those who dare to disobey his commands. The people are forced into the ranks of the League, and a bag of money is made for the defence of a certain set of politicians. These cases can be multiplied *ad infinitum*. They give an excellent illustration of the power and influence of the priest in Irish affairs, and show how easily it can be expanded to cover every department of human life and intercourse.

CHAPTER VI.

ACTION OF THE IRISH PRIESTS IN POLITICS.

THE effect of the claims of the Irish Hierarchy to stand above the law which came into such prominence in 1886 was soon apparent in the language and acts of the priests all over Ireland.

INCENDIARY LANGUAGE OF AN AMERICAN PRIEST.

An American priest, Rev. Mr. Hayes, who introduced himself to a meeting at Youghal during the Keller imbroglio, made use of the following language: "Render a voluntary, prompt, and universal obedience to the behests of the National League, and if this don't free you from the tyrant that is trampling you down, we have something in America to complete the business. The present English atrocities in Ireland are greater crimes against God than the use of dynamite or political assassination to put an end to them. If England and the landlords did the same thing in America, and would despise our appeals for justice, we would, if we could, pelt them, not only with dynamite, but with the lightnings of heaven and the fires of hell, till every British bulldog, whelp, and cur would be pulverised and made topdressing for the soil."*

A reference to the evidence of the Special Commission proves that such language as this has been almost paralleled any time in Ireland since 1879. Here are some samples.

"Cooking the Land-Grabber."

Rev. Mr. Murphy, at Curragh, County Kerry, on Sept. 11th, 1881, said: "We have been fooled out of our rights for the last two hundred years, and it is much better to fight against our enemies on the battlefield than starve in the workhouse. I think the cause has made great progress. One good thing you have done: you have cooked the small land-grabber. He is done brown. But you have got to cook the big land-grabber. I should think there are plenty of night-boys about to see to them."

The "land-grabber" referred to directly was named Brown, which gave particular point to the remark. Nothing could be plainer than this allusion to the connection between "land-grabbing" and the sanction of the moonlight brigade, and even Archbishop Walsh, in his evidence, was obliged to say that the speech was "monstrous."

Again, the evidence of Rev. Mr. Considine, of Ardrahan, County Galway, is interesting, as giving point to the feelings and convictions of the Irish Protes-

* *Daily Express*, Nov. 8th, 1886.

tant minority. This reverend gentleman was president of the branch of the League in his parish. The regular meetings were held in the sacristy of his chapel every Sunday after Mass; and what their deliberations were like may be gathered from the admitted sentiments of Rev. Mr. Considine. He admitted having said on one occasion, "I tell you the wretch who does not join the League, that man deserves to go down to the cold, dead damnation of disgrace." On another occasion Rev. Mr. Considine referred to land-grabbers as renegades, and he had the extraordinary audacity to justify these expressions as moderate, and partaking of the nature of "moral suasion."

A Rebel Priest.

Many other instances of the influence of priests in Irish politics cropped up during the trial, but we may quote a passage from a speech by Rev. Mr. Sheehy (who was mentioned favourably by Archbishop Walsh) as a very good illustration of the inflammatory character of Irish ecclesiastical oratory. On April 12th, 1885, when the Prince and Princess of Wales were in Ireland, great Nationalist demonstrations were held in County Cork for the purpose of protesting against "any parleying with the representatives of foreign rule." Rev. Mr. Sheehy spoke on this occasion at Kilmallock. "There was no need," he said, "for a foreign prince to come to Ireland. The Irish people had nothing to say to the Prince of Wales. He had no connection with the people of Ireland, except that link of the Crown that had been formed for this country, and that was the symbol of Ireland's slavery. He advised the farmers and labourers to be united, and denounced land-grabbing. There was but one land-grabber he liked, and that was the White Czar—this Muscovite gentleman who had put his head over the Afghan border and declared, in violation of all law and order, that he would have that little slice of English territory." At this allusion a voice cried out, " Let the Czar send to Ireland, and he will get plenty of volunteers." It is quite evident that the union of hearts was a sentiment quite strange to Rev. Mr. Sheehy a year before Mr. Gladstone surrendered to Mr. Parnell.

Bound to Bury Them.

At a meeting at Crosspatrick, in County Kilkenny, on Oct. 31st, 1884, attended by Mr. Marum, M.P., Rev. Mr. Duggan, of Kilkenny, speaking of bailiffs and land agents, said: "He could not, of course, recommend them to boycott them, because the Crimes Act was in being now; but he would tell them what they could do. They were not bound to walk with them, or to marry them; but he would tell them what they were bound to do in charity: they were bound to bury them." *

* *Evening Mail*, Oct. 31st, 1884.

The simple moonlighter would naturally infer that before burying began there would have to be some shooting. Why talk of burying without a corpse?

On St. Patrick's Day, 1884, Rev. B. O'Hagan, in company with Mr. W. O'Brien, M.P., went to Newcastle-on-Tyne and made a flaming speech, in which the following passage occurred:—

"They had two classes of landlords, in brief. They had the royal scoundrels who got the confiscated soil of his ancestors. He asked any of these noble ruffians to show him the title by which they laid claim to the land of his forefathers. Then they had the class of landlords who purchased their estates in the Land Courts. But they purchased stolen goods, and they knew that the land was stolen. In the first place, they would have to get rid of the landlords; and, in the second place, they would acquire national independence."

Here both the owner who claimed in descent and the purchaser who bought in open market were equally denounced. What chance would the land question have of being equitably settled in a parliament nominated by such men?

Hell Not Hot Enough.

On Jan. 26th, 1885, Mr. Parnell made a celebrated speech at Milltown-Malbay, County Clare, and the chair was occupied by Rev. P. White, P.P. One of the most violent speeches was made by Rev. Mr. M'Kenna, C.C., who said: "He had been asked to say a few words about land-grabbing. He could not think how it was possible for a land-grabber to be amongst them at the present moment. The land-grabber was a man of whom he would use the words a great Irishman had applied to another class of people, and say that to punish a land-grabber 'hell was not hot enough, nor eternity long enough.'"*

Priests Denounce Poor Law Guardians.

In the year 1887 there was a conference of the Roman Catholic clergy of Cork, Bishop O'Callaghan presiding. After the passing of a resolution against the Crimes Act, the following significant resolution was unanimously adopted:—

"That the action of certain Catholic magistrates of this city, who secured by their votes the election of an avowed Orangeman as chairman of the Cork Board of Guardians, was at variance with Catholic principles, and deserves our strong condemnation."†

What becomes of the free franchises of the ratepayers if a religious body censures individuals for exercising their legal rights? The claim put forward in this by the Roman Catholic Hierarchy is utterly destructive of civil liberty.

* *Freeman's Journal*, Jan. 27th, 1885.
† *Dublin Evening Mail*, April 20th, 1887.

Two Priests Jailed.

In 1888 two priests—Rev. L. Farrelly and Rev. M. Clarke, of Arklow—were prosecuted by the Crown on a charge of unlawfully inciting to an unlawful conspiracy to boycott a Mr. John O'Connor in the ordinary course of his business, and sent to prison for so doing. Their language should be noted. Rev. Mr. Farrelly in a public speech said :—

"My friends, it will not do if you don't hunt the land-grabber and hoot the landlord exterminator. As long as you don't make the place hot for those parties, so long will they reign and rule in your midst. Why, would you give your money to your enemies? It is treason, I think, for any English person to sell ammunition to a power at war with Great Britain. Therefore, it is treason to the Irish cause for you to give money to any one who is not united with your cause. Let him be Protestant or Catholic, and if he be not united with me, none of my money will he ever possess."

Rev. Mr. Clarke used similar language, and referred to the possibility of Mr. O'Connor dying suddenly and without receiving the last rites of his Church. Both priests were found guilty, and the judgment was affirmed on appeal by the Exchequer Division.

A Judge Condemns the Priest of his own Church.

Chief Baron Palles, himself a Roman Catholic, in his

judgment, emphasised the position of the priest in every department of Irish life. He pointed out that Rev. Mr. Farrelly was addressing the people not alone on the subject of the law of the land, but he was referring also to the law of God, of which he was the sacred exponent, and to whose words, as the exponent of the moral law, the people were entitled, and indeed bound, to give reverence almost as if he were the Deity whom he represented. With what subject was he dealing? He was dealing with a question of justice, with a question of truth. And here they found the anointed priest of God, who from his pulpit on Sundays inculcated upon his parishioners the paramount duty of charity and justice to all, telling the people that they ought by combined action to boycott O'Connor, that they ought to join in resolutions for carrying out that object, and make the place too hot for land-grabbers. Of course, an educated man, or a man of intelligence, would be able to separate the two characters which were filled on that occasion by the reverend gentlemen, and to discriminate between Rev. Mr. Farrelly the citizen and Rev. Mr. Farrelly the clergyman; but how could they suppose that the people of the Church of those whom the reverend gentleman was addressing could separate these two characters?

Rev. J. M'Fadden.

No Irish priest, perhaps, has had more publicity than Rev. J. M'Fadden, of Gweedore. He was an advocate of the Plan of Campaign, and urged its adoption on the people in a speech from the altar. He was sentenced on Jan. 30th, 1888, to three months' imprisonment, which was increased on appeal to six months, the judge describing Rev. Mr. M'Fadden's declaration, "I am the law in Gweedore," as an impudent and arrogant assumption. The celebrated Colonel Dopping, who was Captain Hill's agent at Gweedore, thus described a *rencontre* which he had one day on the estate where he was engaged in resuming possession of a small cottage :—

"The door was open, and no one in. I was contemplating the taking of peaceable possession of the premises when Mr. M'Fadden rushed in. I told him civilly he had no right to come in on those lands—that they were in Captain Hill's possession; and I there and then warned him off all lands that were then in Captain Hill's possession. He turned on me in a fury, and called me a 'tyrant and a bully.' I told him if he repeated these remarks I would put him out. He continued, and accordingly I proceeded to endeavour to put him out. Unfortunately for me he had on a waterproof coat or Inverness cape, and when I caught him by the arm I could not retain hold sufficiently to put him out, when he made the remark, 'Take your polluted hands off my consecrated body,' which high-flown language induced the retort, 'Your consecrated body be hanged.' Flesh and blood could not stand this reverend gentleman's impertinence. He was always before me or after me wherever I went, advising or directing the resident magistrates as if they were mere tools of his." *

Colonel Dopping, as Mr. Gladstone knows, is a man of honour and of truth, and the above description is an excellent sketch of Rev. Mr. M'Fadden's tone and manner.

FIREBRAND PRIESTS.

There can be no doubt that the bludgeoning to death of District-Inspector Martin was the result of covert incentives to violence repeated over and over again by the leaders of the Nationalist party in Donegal. Rev. Daniel Stephens, of Falcarragh, in that county, had been sent to jail for breaking the law. On his release from Derry on July 20th, 1888, he returned to his parish amidst great demonstrations of delight. Rev. J. J. Doherty, C.C., who was acting for Rev. Mr. Stephens, addressed the Cloughaneely contingent at the League Rooms, " and told them he was glad to see them all armed with sticks, and assured them if the police used any unnecessary interference he would tell them how to use them.' He then formed the crowd into fours in military order, and marched them off to Dunfanaghy. Later in the day Rev. Daniel Stephens declared "he was as ready for the fray as ever." Another clergyman said the

* *The Union*, Sept. 28th, 1888.

time had come when all people should be treated either as friends or foes, and that a second party could not be tolerated, let alone a third or fourth party, but "all should be cut off like rotten branches." One speaker said that informers should not be tolerated, and that they should not be let live. He assured them that the Irish in America would supply the sinews of war.*

With such language common amongst the clerical leaders of the people in Donegal for six months previous, it is not surprising that an ignorant and superstitious people were inflamed to wreak their vengeance on an officer who dared to attack the "anointed body" of Father M'Fadden.

FATHER M'FADDEN AND THE MURDER OF DISTRICT-INSPECTOR MARTIN.

It was when District-Inspector Martin was engaged in enforcing a warrant of arrest against Father M'Fadden, who had refused to obey a summons under the Crimes Act, that this unfortunate officer was barbarously murdered. The scene was thus described at the time:—

"The reverend gentleman, after the manner of modern Irish patriots, hid himself away when he heard of the issue of the warrant, and the police were obliged to

* *Londonderry Sentinel*, Feb. 7th, 1889.

lie in wait for him for some days before getting an opportunity of enforcing the process of the law. At last he appeared to celebrate Mass in the chapel of Gweedore. When the service was over, he emerged from the chapel accompanied by a crowd, described as a body-guard, three hundred in number. It was a gang of these persons, who, five minutes later, with heavy paling stakes, *literally smashed District-Inspector Martin's head into pieces, cracking his skull from ear to ear, reducing his brains to a pulp, and, in fact, inflicting blows enough to have killed an ox.* He had defended his life as long as he could with his sword against the overwhelming number of his assailants, and sought at last to gain the priest's house, either for shelter or to regain his hold of the escaped prisoner; but the door, at which Miss M'Fadden had stood, was closed the moment her brother, the priest, with the tattered remains of his clerical soutane upon him, entered it, and District-Inspector Martin succumbed to the violence of the mob within a few yards of the house. The few policemen with him did their best to defend themselves and to save him, but in vain, and they were all injured."

Such was the tragical result of the intervention of one priest in politics.

A Holy War.

Throughout Ireland the action of the priests led

the people to believe that a holy war might be waged against the authority. The Commission presided over by Lord Cowper had revealed in 1887 a terrible state of things in Ireland. The National League had obtained the upper hand over the people. Outrage followed disobedience to its commands, and no jury in the country districts dared to convict. The people dared not help the police, and murders were committed with impunity unless witnessed by the police. For the fifteen months ending March 31st, 1887, there were :—

CRIMES.	CONVICTIONS.
11 murders	1
23 cases of firing at the person	1
44 assaults	18
84 outrages on cattle	0
51 cases of firing into dwellings	1
175 cases of injury to property	7
388	28

A Priest's Idea of Crimelessness.

These are facts not be gainsaid, and yet the priesthood did not scruple to declare that there was no need to strengthen the law in the face of increasing crime and intimidation. The usual weekly meeting of the Lixnaw (County Kerry) branch was held on Sunday, April 17th, 1887, the same locality where the brutal murder of Fitzmaurice took place some time later.

Rev. T. Nolan, P.P. (president of the branch), took the chair, and spoke as follows:—

"The Jubilee Coercion Bill is a disgrace to England, with all its renown, its cultivation, and its boasted love of constitutional liberty. We condemn the measure: first, on account of its 'causelessness,' there *being nothing in the shape of disturbance or crime* calling for special legislation; and we condemn it, secondly, on account of its exceptionally wicked nature. If the fiends of hell conspired to frame a law for the complete extirpation of every vestige of liberty, they could not devise a measure better calculated to achieve their infamous object than the Coercion Bill at present before the House of Commons."*

THE PRIESTS ELECT A CORONER.

Even in the field of local politics instances have occurred very recently to show how the civil liberties of the Irish people are interfered with and made the subject of ecclesiastical dictation. Both coroners and poor-law guardians in Ireland are supposed to be elected by the ratepayers. As a matter of fact they are too often nominated by the priests. There was a vacancy for the office of coroner in County Westmeath early in 1892, and seven candidates were in the field, among them being one Protestant, and another a prominent Parnellite. At first Mass in

* *Kerry Weekly Reporter*, April 23rd, 1887.

Mullingar on the Sunday before the election Most Rev. Dr. Nulty referred to the forthcoming election of coroner for County Westmeath. In the course of his remarks his lordship reiterated the statements made by him on Sunday week with regard to political matters. He admitted that Parnellites had some intelligence, but he said they had just that small amount of knowledge which is dangerous. The bishops had spoken on the recent political crisis, and when they did so it was the duty of Roman Catholics to obey and follow them. Parnellites persevering in their present course of action were forfeiting their Catholicity. His lordship then went on to refer to the election of coroner, stating that at all the chapels in the county the feeling of the people was being taken by the priests with regard to the different candidates, and whichever the majority elected the priests would support. Was there ever such a mockery of popular election?

The announcement made by the bishop at first Mass was repeated by the priests at the succeeding Masses, and after last Mass two priests attended in the lecture hall and proceeded to take the votes of the few who attended by some original system of ballot. There are 11,000 voters in the county. Four names out of the list of candidates were only allowed to be voted for by the priest—viz., those of Drs. Shiel, White, and Moorhead, and Mr. Gaynor. The others were omitted, for no stated reason, by Dr. Nulty.*

* *United Ireland*, Feb. 6th, 1892.

Where is the civil and religious liberty of a country where local elections can be treated in such a manner by a Roman Catholic bishop? The Act of Parliament which provides the machinery for ascertaining the opinion of the ratepayers is absolutely nullified by clerical influence. "My mouth," said Bishop Nulty in effect, "shall be the Parliament of England."

PRIESTLY INTIMIDATION AT A POOR-LAW ELECTION.

Again, an inquiry was opened at Castlebar on May 1st, 1892, by the Local Government Board inspector, into allegations of intimidation at a poor-law election, in which a Parnellite named Quinn and an anti-Parnellite named M'Cormack were the candidates. Evidence was given that Rev. Mr. O'Flaherty had said the light of heaven might never shine on those, and they might never prosper on earth, who voted for Quinn. At the collection of dues Rev. Mr. O'Flaherty had asked him whom he was going to vote for. The witness said for Quinn, and then the priest said, "'Take back your money if you are going to vote for Quinn." The witness voted for M'Cormack; but he had intended to vote for Quinn if the priest had not interfered with him. A man who could not write and did not fill in his voting-paper sent it to be filled in by the priest. Others who could not write admitted that they had got the priests to fill up and mark their voting-papers, as if they were illiterate; while a number of voting-papers were not forthcoming at all. The inquiry was postponed for a day to enable the reverend gentleman to complete a deposition he had begun on the first day; but the inspector received a letter from Rev. Mr. O'Flaherty, dated the same day, from the presbytery in the town, saying he could not attend, as he had made other arrangements.*

A Priest Incites to Rebellion.

The attitude of the Irish priesthood towards the law of the land was well illustrated in a letter addressed by Father Arthur Ryan, of Thurles, to the *Tablet*, an English Roman Catholic newspaper, which has invariably opposed the Separatist party. The letter was naturally quoted with great prominence in *United Ireland*, and we give an extract :—

"Ever since the Union the best and most honourable of Irishmen have looked on rebellion as 'a sacred duty,' *provided there were a reasonable chance of success.* It was the absence of this reasonable chance of making rebellion successful that alone bound wise and brave Irishmen to conscientiously oppose armed resistance to the Government of this country. It has never occurred to me to consider acquiescence to the Government of England as a moral obligation or as other than a dire necessity. . . . We have never, thank God, lied to our oppressors by saying we were loyal

* *Daily Express*, June 3rd, 1892.

to them. And when we have condemned the rebels whose heroism and whose self-sacrifice we have loved and wept over, we condemned, not their want of loyalty, but their want of prudence. We thought it wrong to plunge the land into the horrors of war with no hope of success. But, in common with humanity itself, we have rejected what O'Connell led himself to say if not to think—that the liberty of our country is not worth our blood if our blood could win it."

The apostle of peace then goes on to give a reasoned defence of the Plan of Campaign on the avowed ground that it is an act of insurrection :—

"If, then, the Legislature in London, having declined to protect the homes and property of the tenants in Ireland, and the Government having, despite soft words, threatened brute force and imprisonment, its time-worn plan of campaign, against us; if, under these circumstances, we find that our new plan in self-defence is likely to succeed,—why should we care whether it be an act of rebellion or not? Its chance of success is, indeed, all we look to. Rebellion, with the chance of being successful, rebellion against tyrannous misgovernment, is, the wide world over, a sacred duty. Englishmen have blessed it in their own case—in the case of every nation except Ireland. Irishmen bless it, and Irish priests and Irish bishops bless it, and declare it to be high and unassailable morality—a holy war in the cause of the poor and oppressed, a struggle for hearths and homes. Rebels we are, almost to a man, against the injustice and misgovernment, the hollow mockery, we see and touch on every side, but which our pious critics cannot or will not recognise. True, we have been up to this 'inopportunists' in the matter of rebellion; but now our opportunity has come, and we give our glad 'God-speed' to what promises to be, at long last, a successful plan of campaign. Whether or not that plan be constitutional may be an interesting question of politics, but it is no question of morals."*

A Priest Assists a Prisoner to Break Prison Rules.

These are only a few samples from the bulk of priestly dictation, arrogance, and turbulence in Ireland. They could be indefinitely multiplied. Priests broke the law of the land in every conceivable manner. Several were dismissed from their posts as chaplains to prisons because they smuggled out communications from the lawbreakers to the Press. Even Mr. Conybeare, M.P., an English member, did not scruple to use a priest for this object.† Nothing was left by

---

* *United Ireland*, Jan. 1st, 1887.

† "On Tuesday, Rev. John Doherty, Adm., the Catholic chaplain of Derry Prison, was dismissed from the office by the written order of the Prisons Board. It appears that during last month several letters were published in some English newspapers relating to the prison treatment of Mr. Conybeare, M.P., and under the signature of that gentleman,

them undone for six years to make the Government of Ireland impossible. Failing in that unscrupulous and scandalous task, they have only injured the religion which they profess, and brought contempt upon the sacred calling of the religious teacher.

This harsh verdict must perforce be given of the great majority of the Irish priesthood. That a small minority existed in Ireland who loathed and abhorred the practices of the League, and the part taken by their brethren in carrying them out, need hardly be stated. The Bishop of Limerick denounced the Plan of Campaign as "politically foolish and morally wrong." Individual priests throughout Ireland have had the courage of their convictions, and spoke out God's truth with regard to boycotting fearlessly and plainly to the people. Peradventure if there had been a few more such in the high places of the hierarchy, Ireland might have been spared the scourges and plagues which have

who is at present undergoing a sentence of four months' imprisonment in the jail. These letters came under the notice of the Prisons Board, and an inspector, Mr. Joyce, was instructed to hold an inquiry as to how the letters reached the newspapers in which they appeared. On August 31st the inspector arrived at the prison and sent a note to Father Doherty, asking him to meet him at the jail for a few moments. Father Doherty accordingly called, and was informed that the business on which he was required was to give evidence on oath in reference to certain letters appearing in the *Star* newspaper over the signature of Mr. C. A. V. Conybeare, M.P. 'I will answer no questions,' said the chaplain."—*Freeman's Journal*, Sept. 11th, 1889.

made her a by-word amongst the nations, and brought her into her present chaotic plight. But facts are facts, and history must be written to square with the rule and not with the exception. The priests in Irish politics have been a scandal for many years, and their cloth must be judged by the public acts done under its shelter and sanction.

CHAPTER VII.

THE PARNELL DIVORCE CASE—AND AFTER.

ON Nov. 17th, 1890, the verdict in the divorce action of O'Shea *v.* O'Shea and Parnell was given. Ten months had elapsed between the issue of the writ and the trial; and as the charges in general form had been for nearly a year before the public, it is quite certain that even in the sublimated atmosphere of the Irish Hierarchy some speculation must have taken place as to what effect an adverse verdict might have upon the political situation. The actual result, as we know it, can be traced to several causes.

CAUSES OF THE REVOLT AGAINST MR. PARNELL'S LEADERSHIP.

The most powerful, no doubt, was what has been called "the Nonconformist conscience." The secondary causes were undoubtedly the recent disaffection towards Mr. Parnell of the Church of Rome at home and abroad, and of a considerable section of his own followers. Mr. Parnell, a Protestant, had beaten the Irish Hierarchy and the priesthood on their own ground. He was their master, and they knew it. Chafe as they might in secret, they had found it absolutely necessary to acknowledge his power and authority, and the very last sign of submission had been to deliver into the hands of the Protestant leader the care in Parliament of Roman Catholic education. What Cardinal M'Cabe would have thought of this final step we can easily judge. In 1881 Mr. Parnell went to Paris, and was entertained at dinner by Victor Hugo, M. Henri Rochefort, M. Lockroy, and other avowed haters of priests and admirers of Garibaldi. In a Lenten pastoral the cardinal deplored this occurrence. "A calamity," he said, "more terrible and humiliating than any that has yet befallen Ireland seems to threaten our people to-day. Allies for this country in her struggle for justice are sought from the ranks of impious infidels, who have plunged their own unhappy land into misery, who are sworn to destroy the foundations of all religions. Will Catholic Ireland tolerate such an indignity? Will she give her confidence to men who have wickedly planned it? Will she break from all the holy traditions which during ages commanded for her the veneration of the Christian world? Let us pray that God in His mercy may forbid it."*

The late Cardinal's queries have all been answered by Archbishop Walsh in the affirmative. He not only tolerated the Parnellite indignity; he bowed to the

* *Daily Telegraph*, Feb. 23rd, 1881.

Parnell whirlwind; subscribed to Nationalist testimonials, accepted the associate of Atheists and Communists, placed the care of Catholic education in his hands, and trusted to the chapter of accidents to enable him to carry out his aims and objects in the future. Nay more, the Irish priest in almost every parish in the country became the willing henchman of Mr. Parnell, and until the hierarchy decided what course to pursue was by no means certain what line to adopt when the decision in the O'Shea case was flashed to every village in Ireland.

The verdict was delivered on Nov. 17th, 1890, and the dramatic incidents that followed will not easily be forgotten. At first the whole of Mr. Parnell's followers remained outwardly loyal to him. In Dublin the National League met on the 19th, and the Irish party expressed their unswerving allegiance to their leader. On the same day Messrs. W. O'Brien, M.P., and T. P. O'Connor, M.P., at that time in America, cabled their resolve to keep Mr. Parnell at the head of the party. Two days later, on Nov. 20th, a great meeting was held in the Leinster Hall, Dublin, at which Mr. Justin M'Carthy, M.P., and Mr. T. Healy, M.P., moved and seconded a resolution declaring that Mr. Parnell possessed the confidence of the Irish nation, and that the whole party would stand by their leader.

Mr. Healy stated at the time to Mr. Harrington, M.P., that he had been to County Meath immediately after the verdict was published, and had seen Bishop Nulty on the subject. The prelate told Mr. Healy that the only course open to the Irish party was to stick to Mr. Parnell.* A convention in County Meath, largely attended by priests, and other public meetings, gave their adherence to Mr. Parnell's leadership. On Nov. 25th Mr. Parnell was re-elected in London chairman of the party by a unanimous vote, amid much handshaking and vows of continued allegiance. Up to this date, eight days after the verdict had been published, the Roman Catholic Hierarchy had said not a word in public.

The Nationalist cat had jumped to Mr. Parnell. Would he carry the day even now, as he had done against the Pope in 1883? Archbishop Walsh decided to wait a little longer. "There are few dangers," he wrote subsequently in defence, "more seriously to be avoided than precipitancy in action." Especially, it may be remarked, when you do not know exactly what to do.

The Ecclesiastical Cat Jumps.

Then came Mr. Gladstone's letter of Nov. 26th. The Old Parliamentary Hand, ever since the verdict, had been feeling with tender care and solicitude the pulse of the Nonconformist body throughout Great Britain. The National Liberal Federation was sitting

---

* *National Independent*, Dec. 13th, 1892.

at Sheffield by a lucky coincidence on the Thursday and Friday after the verdict, and Mr. Gladstone, no doubt, received both light and leading from that august body. On Sunday, Nov. 23rd, the Nonconformist chapel bell rang in tones not to be denied, and the sacrifice of Mr. Parnell instantly came within the "range of practical politics." The pirate captain must walk the plank he had so often prepared for others. On Saturday, the 29th, Mr. Parnell's manifesto appeared. The following Wednesday, Dec. 3rd, sixteen days after the verdict of the Divorce Court, after the whole moral conscience of the Protestant Church had revolted and expressed its opinion, the Roman Catholic Hierarchy in Ireland pronounced an opinion on the subject. The terms of the address are remarkable. It declared that Mr. Parnell was not fit to be the leader of the Irish people. "As pastors of the Catholic nation, we do not base this judgment and solemn declaration on political grounds," said the bishops; but they went on to contradict their own saving clause. "We cannot but be influenced," said the bishops' address, "by the conviction that the continuance of Mr. Parnell as a leader of even a section of the Irish party must have the effect of disorganising our ranks, and ranging, as in hostile camps, the hitherto united forces of our country. Confronted with the prospects of contingencies so disastrous, we see nothing but inevitable defeat at the approaching general election, and, as a result, Home Rule indefinitely postponed, coercion perpetuated, the hands of the evictor strengthened, and the tenants already evicted without a shadow of a hope of ever being restored to their homes."*

The main point in this address may not be political, but it reads very like it. If Mr. Parnell was retained as leader, the Liberal party would be defeated at the general election. That seems the ordinary inference. Mr. Parnell adopted that line, and Sir Charles Russell himself has confessed that such was the actuating motive of the Irish Hierarchy. In any case there can be no doubt that there was singular delay on the part of the bishops in denouncing Mr. Parnell's moral delinquency.

The Hierarchy and Mr. W. O'Brien's Breeches.

How did they act on a former occasion not of transcendent importance? On Saturday, Feb. 2nd, 1889, the *Freeman's Journal* announced in large type " the outrage on Mr. O'Brien's breeches." The *Freeman* of Monday, Feb 4th, contained " a noble protest from the Irish Hierarchy," signed by twenty-six bishops and archbishops, denouncing the Government in the following language for "this infamous outrage":—

"We, the undersigned archbishops and bishops of Ireland, feel imperatively called upon to join in a solemn protest against the shameful indignities and inhuman violence which, as we have learned, have been

* *Freeman's Journal*, Dec. 4th, 1891.

inflicted upon Mr. William O'Brien, M.P., in Clonmel Jail, to the manifest peril of his life and the danger of the public peace. In the interest alike of humanity and order we deem it our duty to declare that Her Majesty's Government should not suffer a moment to be lost in securing the discontinuance of maltreatment, which is shocking to adherents of all political parties and opposed to the usages of civilisation." *

It took the Irish bishops forty-eight hours in 1889 to get out a protest against the Conservative Government about the rape of Mr. O'Brien's breeches, while they waited sixteen days before drafting and signing a political manifesto, denouncing what they called "the shocking infamy laid bare to the world by the reported evidence of the O'Shea divorce case."

The Parnellite View of the Situation.

The question whether the ecclesiastical demonstration was a moral or a political move has been trenchantly dealt with by Mr. Parnell's followers.

Mr. E. Leamy, M.P., addressing the Central National League from the chair on March 10th, dealt at length with the positions of the archbishops and bishops. He said :—

"Let the bishops make up their minds as to what is the real character of our offence before they condemn us. They offer an excuse for remaining silent for

* *Freeman's Journal*, Feb. 4th, 1889.

weeks, some couple of weeks, after the Divorce Court proceedings were published. Yet during these weeks Ireland was rallying to the standard of the chief, who up to that time was assailed only by Englishmen and the colleagues who, at the bidding of Englishmen, had deserted him. During that time you, and men like you throughout the country, were meeting at the Boards of Guardians and the Town Commissioners' rooms everywhere. In your National League you were all pledging your fidelity to Parnell. If you are guilty of a crime in standing by him now, you were guilty of a crime in standing by him then; and I ask the Irish bishops how can they claim to be the watchful guardians of the people's morals, how can they claim to be the men whom we are to look to in trust and confidence, if they could stand idly by for a whole fortnight when their nation was running to perdition and ruin?"*

Whatever the motive reason, the fact remains that once the Irish Hierarchy put their hand to the plough they never looked back. The most unsparing crusade was preached against the Parnellite party. It was quite clear that if Mr. Parnell could be driven out of politics, Archbishop Walsh would hold the key of the situation. The private enemies of the Irish leader joined hands with the clergy. Then came scenes in Committee Room 15, and a plan of campaign was soon mapped out. The *mot d'ordre* went out that all who supported Mr. Parnell and his candidates opposed the

* *Freeman's Journal*, March 11th, 1891.

Church. The struggle was based on a question of morals. It was a sin to go against the Church in a matter of morals, and all who did so were sinners, and must be dealt with accordingly. How the campaign was carried out remains to be seen.

CHAPTER VIII.

THE PRIEST AT BYE-ELECTIONS.

THE KILKENNY ELECTION, 1890.

IT was not long before the two new factions in Irish politics which sprang out of the great political divide of 1890 found a battlefield on which to expend their fury. Mr. Marum, the member for North Kilkenny, died suddenly. Sir John Pope Hennessy was put forward as the priests' candidate, and Mr. Vincent Scully as Mr. Parnell's choice. Both were Roman Catholics—both were Nationalists; and the result was everywhere regarded as a trial of strength. The Roman Catholic Hierarchy gave their orders, and ecclesiastical electioneering was reduced to a pitch of scientific accuracy seldom before equalled, though it has been subsequently excelled. The *modus operandi* of the election was admirably described by the *Star* special correspondent, who may be taken as a hostile witness :—

THE "STAR" ON BLACK-COATED ELECTIONEERING.

"The note of this Irish election is not devilment,

but black-coated electioneering. There has been plenty of this. The most interesting electioneering reminiscence in the *Star* man's life is the sight of Canon Cody, the parish priest of Castlecomer, standing at the door of the principal polling-booth taking voters in hand as they came up to record their votes, and impressing on each as he entered a last word of paternal instruction. It was a great spectacle. . . . At Ballyragget, voters, as they came up to the station, were taken into the priest's house for the last word of good counsel. At Johnstown the priest was in the booth. All over the division priests acted as personation agents. At Gowran each of three personation agents was in a black frock. In the electoral history of the world there is registered no device compared with this. Voters found the priest so all-pervading that some of them must have believed a ballot-box itself to be an ecclesiastical appurtenance with a priest inside it." *

On the Sunday before the poll, from the altar, clad in their sacred robes, priests threatened those who dared to vote on the morrow for Vincent Scully. Within the precincts of every chapel premises, save two or three, in the constituency they held meetings in support of Pope Hennessy, and in some cases warned the voters to vote for him if they would escape never-ending pain. The preachers of Sunday were Sir John Pope Hennessy's personation agents on the Monday. Every

* *Star*, Dec. 23rd, 1890.

illiterate voter was obliged to declare in their presence the candidate for whom he wished to vote. They were led up in batches to the booths by their clergymen; they were received inside by clergymen; and in the presence of clergymen they voted for Pope Hennessy. The result of the poll was in accordance with the preparations. The priests' candidate was elected by a majority of 1171.

A Priest Claims Immunity from Eviction for Non-payment of Rent.

Mr. Vincent Scully, the defeated candidate at the Kilkenny election, has published a pamphlet which gives a curious account of the conduct of the parish priest of Golden, County Tipperary, in the matter of paying rent for his house. In 1875 Father M'Donnell was appointed to the parish, and he became tenant to Mr. Scully of a house and garden at an annual rent of £20. In a few years the reverend gentleman wrote complaining that the rent was excessive. No reduction was given, and in 1885 Father M'Donnell returned Mr. Scully's "Christmas offering" of £5, which he described as "too paltry and too shabby" for his acceptance. In 1888 Mr. Scully's "Christmas dues" were also rejected. In December 1889 the nominal rent of 2s. a year charged for Golden Chapel, which was nine years in arrear, was demanded, to which Father M'Donnell replied, "I enclose you 18s.—Mr. Scully's rent for the house of God." The money was, however, refunded next day. In 1890 the dispute was submitted to Mr. W. O'Brien, M.P., by Mr. Scully, but Mr. O'Brien passed it on to the Archbishop of Cashel. The Archbishop's terms were accepted by Mr. Scully, but Father M'Donnell refused to accept them, as he "knew perfectly well that the award was given by what is called by jugglers the trick of legerdemain." He added: "Mr. Scully intends to become a second Smith-Barry in the country. He should not become a fellow-tourist in England with Canon Keller and William O'Brien, denouncing Ponsonby and Smith-Barry for refusing arbitration to their tenants, and repudiate and turn his back on it at his own door when he himself is concerned." Writing in August last, when the eviction proceedings were pending, Father M'Donnell said: "No parish priest of the arch-diocese of Cashel was ever evicted from his house since the days of Oliver Cromwell. It will remain then for you, Mr. Scully, an advanced Nationalist and an ardent Home Ruler, to break that long record, and that without a just cause. When you evict me, you will also evict our Divine Lord in the Blessed Sacrament." Since the eviction nobody has offered to rent Mr. Scully's house and garden.*

SLIGO ELECTION.

Meanwhile, clerical boycotting went on all over Ireland. Parnellites were visited in the name of religion with spiritual and in some cases temporal

* See *Times*, Oct. 10th, 1892.

penalties. In some dioceses the sacraments were refused to them. In others members of Parnell leadership committees were denounced from the pulpit as members of secret societies condemned by the Church. In Belfast public prayers were offered up at the altar against them, and they were compelled to listen in silence. In the diocese of Meath the Easter offerings of some were returned to them.

Soon another vacancy took place. Mr. Macdonald, the member for North Sligo, died in March 1891, and another bitter contest took place. Determined to push their advantage to the utmost, the priests adopted the the same tactics, and with a similar result. In spite or Mr. Parnell's personal presence and active superintendence, Mr. V. Dillon, the Independent candidate, was beaten by Mr. B. Collery, a local grocer, unknown to fame, but the priests' nominee, by a majority of 765.

CARLOW ELECTION.

The Carlow election, in July 1891, was a remarkable instance of the power of the priests and the unscrupulous manner in which it was wielded. The anti-Parnellite or Federation candidate was Mr. Hammond, a grocer in the town of Carlow, with nothing to commend save his respectability and sound Catholicity. The Parnellite candidate was Mr. Andrew Kettle, an original member of the old Land League, and well known in Irish politics for many years. One priest, Rev. Mr. O'Neill, of Bagenalstown, had given his support to Mr. Kettle; but his action was soon nipped in the bud. On a complaint being made to Bishop Lynch, that Roman Catholic prelate wrote the following letter:—

"ST. PATRICK'S COLLEGE,
"*June 23rd*, 1891.

"DEAR FATHER NORRIS,—I have written to Father O'Neill to abstain from all opposition, directly or indirectly, privately or publicly, to the Federation candidate, and to permit his curates or any priest with their approval to attend meetings, and in every way to promote the cause espoused by the bishops in this unhappy crisis. With all blessings, ever faithfully yours,

"JAMES LYNCH,
"✠ *Bishop of Kildare and Leighlin.*"

Can a more glaring illustration of political and spiritual coercion be imagined? It means that the Roman Catholic Hierarchy not only claim, but actually exercise, plenary powers of veto over the political opinions of the priesthood, and that, therefore, the views of the hierarchy are supreme and final. In this case Bishop Lynch gave his priesthood directions and full liberty withal to promote "in every way" the candidature of one faction, while he gagged by letter the only priest who seemed to have had the smallest political independence. If a priest could thus be treated, what can be expected in the case of laymen?

The result was a foregone conclusion. There was an overwhelming majority for Mr. Hammond, and he sits now as the "representative" of County Carlow. In effect, he is merely the nominee of Bishop Lynch and the pliant tool of the Roman Catholic hierarchy. No such spectacle can be imagined in England by any exercise of the imagination. But it is a remarkable proof that it is possible in Ireland for the politics of that country to be controlled by thirty eminent individuals, who have been placed by the Pope of Rome in command of the consciences and the civil and religious opinions of the Roman Catholic community in that country.

Politics from the Altar.

Protests were not wanting on the part of the Parnellite faction against this despotic action of the priesthood in Carlow. At a public meeting in Dublin on July 14th, 1891, Mr. Leamy gave the following interesting experiences of the Carlow election:—

" He was present himself at a Mass, and the priest at the post Communion, standing on the altar steps, addressing the people, read out the political letter of the bishop, which dealt solely with the political action of Mr. Parnell, and which contained no reference to the moral question, and he read the names of the bishops with their full titles, and then he proceeded to comment upon the letter, and, of course, he expressed the hope that the people would not vote for the nominee of Mr.

Parnell. Well, perhaps all that was very fair electioneering, but he followed that up by this statement: 'They have brought down Orangemen to this country,' he said, 'and these gentlemen are anxious that the election should be over speedily, for they want to get back to the North for July 12th, to attack the Roman Catholic chapels.' Now, that was a statement made by a priest, which they all knew was utterly without foundation, and he should say that he was astonished to hear a priest, when he had the very hearts of the people in his hand, standing upon the altar steps making a statement completely at variance to the truth as that, and which could not have had any other effect than that of exciting the passions of an ignorant people, for intelligent people would not heed such language against a section of their fellow-countrymen."

Mr. Leamy's admission that the vast majority of the Carlow electors are ignorant is remarkable, for County Carlow has always had the reputation of being one of the most civilised counties in Ireland, where crime and outrage during the worst period of the land war were almost unknown. If the Carlow electors are ignorant, what must be the state of the electors of the more backward parts of Ireland?

Mediævalism Revived.

Mr. James Dalton, M.P., also dealt with the question of priestly intimidation, and made some statements, which, had they been made by a Unionist on English platforms, would hardly be believed. He said:—

"A good deal has been said of the influence exercised by the priests at the election in Carlow. They had exercised that influence ten times harder than at either Sligo or Kilkenny. The bishops had actually a few days before the election issued a political manifesto. Fancy the bishops meeting at Maynooth to look after their spiritual well-being, and sending out simply an electioneering dodge. Without saying anything disrespectful, he might at least say that it was a very undignified thing to send out placards to be posted upon all the roads and hedges and ditches of Carlow for the election. The priests said it was all very well, but that they (the Parnellites) had been content to take their support during the past ten or eleven years. Yes, they were content to take their support, but now the other side had the influence of their intimidation. That was what it amounted to. They went so far as to *tell people that their pigs or cattle would die if they did not vote in a certain way.* That was what they were doing now, and it was certainly anything but fair warfare to tell a man that if he did not vote in one way it would interfere with his eternal salvation."*

What a picture is here painted by hands well acquainted with the inwardness of the subject! Can

* *Carlow Sentinel*, July 18th, 1892.

any influences be conceived more contrary to the elementary conceptions of Christianity? How can civil and religious liberty co-exist with such a system of political and spiritual coercion? Mr. Morley, at the National Liberal Club before the general election of 1892, alluding to the Ulstermen, asked, "What are these men afraid of? I never can get an answer to this question."

The answer, or part of it, is given in the speeches of Parnellite Home Rulers themselves. It is because Archbishop Walsh and the authorities of the Roman Catholic Church in Ireland claim and exercise jurisdiction in the political arena, and because under Mr. Gladstone's bill their jurisdiction will be increased and extended.

Cork Election, 1891.

The next bye-election in which the priesthood, breviary in hand, took a prominent part was that of Cork, in November 1891, on the death of Mr. Parnell. The scenes of tumult and violence in this election were almost unparalleled. Mr. Dillon was violently assaulted, and practically civil war was going on for several days. The candidates were Mr. John Redmond, M.P., and Mr. Flavin, a Cork butter merchant, who was recommended to the electors as "The Pope's man." A certain Canon O'Mahony figured prominently in the electoral contest, defying Mr. Redmond and his friends to set foot in his parish. The challenge was accepted, and Mr. Redmond and Mr. John O'Connor, M.P., led a considerable crowd, accompanied by bands, from Cork to Blackrock. There they were met by an opposing crowd, and were attacked with sticks, stones, and mud; but, after a short but desperate encounter, the **aggressive** party were driven off, many of their number disfigured and bleeding. The Parnellites then held a successful meeting, and subsequently returned to Cork exceedingly jubilant.

Absolving Voters from Promises.

Canon O'Mahony had resort to action, which proved that the priesthood were resolved to use every means, both fair and foul, to attain their end. "I have already stated on a former occasion," said this minister of the Gospel, "that those who made promises to vote for Mr. Redmond are not morally bound by the promise."

To show the extent to which priestly dictation was carried in the ward, a rather aged man was about to enter one of the booths, when a personating agent asked him his name. The man stared at him vacantly for a few seconds, and then said, "I will run and ask my priest." He returned again, and showing some doubt as to whether "O" should be prefixed to his name or not, he went again and consulted his adviser. As another old man approached a priest accosted him and asked him if he could read and write. On receiving a negative answer, the clergyman took him by the arm, and in spite of the efforts of some of Mr. Redmond's friends, he led him to the entrance of the polling-booth, and did not lose sight of him until he appeared to be satisfied. He was in the hands of Mr. Flavin's friends.

Bulldozing the Electors.

The result was a foregone conclusion. The "Pope's man" was elected by a majority of 1513, which was almost exactly reproduced at the general election. Mr. W. Redmond, M.P., after the declaration of the poll, stated at Cork :—

"They were beaten because their priests left their churches and their own business to enter into politics and bulldoze the electors of Cork. They opposed Parnell because of what they called his moral crime. There was no moral crime against his (Mr. Redmond's) brother or himself, and he said while as Catholics they respected the priests, and were ready to defend them, they said that in political matters they had no right to dictate to the people how they should vote. If they allowed dictation from the priests, the people of England would never give them Home Rule." *

Mr. John Redmond turned the tables upon the clerical interest shortly after in Waterford, where Mr. Davitt performed the never-to-be-forgotten feat of

* *Cork Constitution*, Nov. 9th, 1891.

refusing to stand until he was knocked down. The contest was an exceedingly bitter one; but in spite of every form of clerical persuasion and intimidation, the Parnellite leader obtained a majority of 546, which was, however, somewhat reduced at the general election.

CHAPTER IX.

THE GENERAL ELECTION, 1892.

WE have now traced the issue of the clerical conspiracy since 1885. The climax came in 1892 at the general election, when the whole force of the Roman Catholic hierarchy was mobilised and used as an overwhelming campaign force in every parish in Ireland. At the Cork election, in July 1892, the Roman Catholic priesthood went to work in a business-like manner to carry the "Pope's men," as they were called—viz., Mr. William O'Brien, M.P., and Mr. M. Healy, M.P. Mr. W. Redmond, M.P., and Mr. Hogan were the Parnellite candidates. The plan of campaign was simple, but effective, and consisted in declarations by the priests that it was a sin to stand by Mr. Parnell's teachings, and a "mortal sin of the deepest dye" to vote for Mr. Parnell's Independent party.

A CRIME TO VOTE AGAINST THE PRIESTS' CANDIDATE.

The leader of the new crusade, the modern Peter the Hermit, was Canon O'Mahony, whose conduct at the bye-election has come already under review. His declaration of principles deserves to be set down in full.

Speaking at a public meeting in the Old Market Place, Cork, on June 27th, 1892, in presence of Mr. William O'Brien and Mr. M. Healy, he said :—

"The question is not whether one political system shall prevail over another, for the Factionists have no fixed political system—you might as well talk of the fixed colour of the chameleon. The question is whether a source of blackguardism and demoralisation is to continue in our midst, or be crushed out by the indignation of conscientious men. I say, therefore, that it is a crime against the law of God, a crime against conscience, to vote for Factionism, or to give it any support whatever. This is not my opinion; it is not merely that of the other clergymen in this city; but is the opinion of the bishop of this diocese, who feels the deepest anxiety to see such a source of demoralisation existing, which is sapping the foundations of religion and morality in the minds of the young. Now, I am glad to say that, if there are any unfortunate persons in this city who don't realise it, it is very well realised throughout this great county of Cork. Speaking to the delegates from the different parts of the county at the late county convention, I am glad to see that everywhere the greatest indignation and abhorrence are evinced against the leaders of faction in this city, and against every one who identified himself with it, even to the extent of signing their nomination papers on the last election occasion." *

* *Cork Herald*, June 28th, 1892.

A Mortal Sin to Vote for Redmond.

Again, speaking on July 5th, in Cork, on the Grand Parade, referring to an attack made upon Mr. William O'Brien, Canon O'Mahony said :—

"In view of this further development of Parnellism, I wonder is there any one in this city who thinks that it was going too far to say it was a crime, a sin, a mortal sin of the deepest dye, to vote for them or to support them in any way ? I am sure if any of you were to be so misguided as to vote for those, or even to fail in doing your utmost against them, you would look back upon your action or omission with sentiments of the deepest remorse hereafter. In the first place, we must hold responsible for this crime all those who signed the nomination papers of John Redmond last November, all those who canvassed for him, and all those who voted for him, for even there the evil character of this Parnellism was evident to any reflecting man. It had perpetrated deeds which ought to make any man see its immoral nature. It had shown itself to be a bad tree that could only bring forth bad fruit. But whatever was the responsibility of those who, by their action last November, helped to perpetuate and give life to this infamous cause, still greater is the responsibility of the men who, with the knowledge of what Parnellism has done since, deliberately again resolved that they would publicly affix their names to the nomination papers, canvass for them, and vote." *

* *Cork Herald*, July 6th, 1892.

An Eye-opening Correspondence between Priest and Politician.

Out of these speeches an interesting correspondence arose between Canon O'Mahony and Mr. W. Redmond, the Parnellite candidate. Mr. W. Redmond declared that the Canon's statement must have an enormous effect upon the minds of hundreds of poor and illiterate people who are deeply devoted to their religion.

"There is no use," he said, "in concealing the fact that if language of this kind is used by gentlemen in the position of Canon O'Mahony, there is an absolute end to freedom of conscience in political matters." *

Writing to Canon O'Mahony, Mr. Redmond put the following categorical questions:—

"Does the Catholic Church forbid, or does it not, the Catholic people of Ireland to support the Independent parliamentary party?"

"Does the Catholic Church forbid its members to vote for Independent candidates?"

"Could any confessor refuse absolution, for this reason only, to a penitent who told him he had made up his mind to vote for the Independent candidate?" †

The following, after much fencing, is Canon O'Mahony's reply, addressed to the *Cork Examiner*:—

"Mr. Redmond, having complained strongly in a former letter that I stated that 'to support the Par-

* *Cork Examiner*, July 4th, 1892.
† For full text see *Dublin Independent*, July 26th, 1892.

nellite party was a crime against the law of God,' at the close of the same letter asked me did I mean to say it was a sin. I really thought I might be excused from the trouble of gravely informing him that a crime was a sin. He also asked whether it was forbidden by the Church, and would involve exclusion from the Sacraments. Without crediting him with any remarkable reasoning power, I did expect that he would be able to make a very obvious inference without assistance. Surely he cannot have succeeded in persuading himself that any one prepared to support the programme of violence with which factionism has been hitherto identified, and which Mr. Harrington officially recommended about a month ago, is in a fit state to receive the Sacraments of the Church."*

Now, although it may suit Mr. Redmond to say, as he did, that his antagonist ran away from his guns, no one who reads Canon O'Mahony's reply can fail to see that he reasserts his assertion that it is a sin to vote for Mr. W. Redmond's supporters, and, further, that any one who did so was in an unfit state to receive the Sacraments of the Church. Let him then be Anathema—is the logical and necessary conclusion. The result of the poll sufficiently proves that the vast majority of the Cork electors believed this to be the upshot of the canon's oratory, for in the city which elected Mr. Parnell unopposed in 1886 his followers were defeated by a majority of 1573.

* *Cork Examiner*, June 29th, 1892.

Mr. Corbet's Farewell to Civil Liberty.

Well did Mr. Corbet, himself a Roman Catholic, and a Parnellite member for many years, express himself after his defeat in his farewell adress to the electors of East Wicklow :—

"In Ireland the Ballot Act and the extension of the franchise have not secured freedom of election. There is no use mincing matters. Under episcopal and clerical influence the exercise of the franchise has become a mockery and a farce ; and unless a rescript from Rome, or, failing that, an Act of Parliament from Westminster, puts a stop to the personal interference of priests at elections, save as regards the exercise of their own legitimate civil rights, Mr. Speaker might *just as well issue his writs to the Roman Catholic archbishops and bishops* of Ireland instead of to the high sheriffs, and the franchise might as well be confined to the clergy themselves." *

A Present to a Priest of Five Hundred Votes.

Mr. John O'Connor was defeated at the general election in South Tipperary by Mr. Mandeville, M.P., and his defeat demonstrates the truth of a proposition freely advanced in that division during the contest, that if a broomstick were nominated by the Roman Catholic priesthood it would sweep any division in Ireland. Mr. John O'Connor himself gave a graphic

* *Cork Examiner*, July 5th, 1892.

description of the way in which the priesthood worked against him. "I find," he said, "that in those districts where the priests of the parish allowed the people to vote according to their consciences I have a majority. But in Ardfinan and Tipperary they have delivered speeches from the pulpit calling upon the people under pains and penalties to vote against me. One priest— Rev. Mr. O'Dwyer, of Solehead—came in here and said to my opponent, 'Here are five hundred votes for you.' He makes a present of them to my opponent, just as he would pass over any property, such as a lot of sheep, from one person to another. . . . If we do not stand together and organise, it would be just as well to abandon all representation, to give up the sham and mockery, and hand over an emasculated Ireland to the bishops and priests of the country. Let us abandon our votes, and let us ask the bishops and priesthood of Ireland to nominate a certain number of members according to their right, and return them to Parliament."

ORGANISED INTIMIDATION OF INDEPENDENT OPINION.

At a meeting of the National League in Dublin on July 27th, 1892, Mr. W. Redmond declared that he did not see the slightest difference between a resident magistrate of Mr. Balfour coming to an election meeting with fifty or one hundred police to charge and break the people's heads—he did not see the slightest difference between that and the actions of the priests who came, not with policemen, but with two or three hundred organised men with sticks in their hands and stones in their pockets to break up their meetings, to put down free speech and inflict summary punishment upon the head of any unfortunate man who dared to hold an independent opinion, or intended to vote for an Independent candidate. If there was a difference at all, it was altogether in favour of the resident magistrate and the police; but to see priests in different parts of Ireland leaving the confessionals and leading mobs of people, knocking down old men, stating that it was sinful to vote for an Independent candidate, and insinuating that people who so voted could not be attended in their dying moments —such a state of affairs, in his opinion, called for more prompt action upon their part than even the abolition of Castle rule in Ireland.*

A Priest Knocks Down Colonel Nolan, M.P.

During the North Galway election in July 1892, the contest between Colonel Nolan, M.P., the Parnellite candidate, and the priests' nominee, Dr. Tanner, was marked by much violence and rioting, in which the clergy took a prominent part. Rev. Michael Heaney was summoned in the following August by the constabulary to answer a charge of aggravated and unprovoked attack upon Colonel Nolan in the streets

* *Dublin Mail*, August 12th, 1892.

of Headford on July 1st, when the latter was carrying on his canvass for the representation of the division. On that occasion Rev. Mr. Heaney, without any warning, came up to the colonel, and felled him to the ground with a fierce blow of a stick. The candidate was covered with blood, and had to retire to the house of a supporter to have his wounds dressed. Colonel Nolan refused to prosecute, but the police authorities were obliged to take note of the peculiar conceptions entertained by Rev. Mr. Heaney on political amenities. There was practically no defence. The pacific representative of the Pope in Ireland admitted the charge, and the bench leniently decided to allow the defendant out on his own bail of £50, to come up for judgment when called upon.

Leading a Storming Party.

Another priest, Rev. Mark Eagleton, was sent for trial on August 11th, together with eight laymen, on a charge of having engaged in a riot in the town of Tuam on June 29th, 1892. A platform, it seems, had been erected in the town for the purposes of one of the two rival factions, who entered into a quarrel for its possession and use. Evidence was given to show that Dr. Tanner, M.P., and Rev. Mr. Eagleton led a storming party, and captured the platform.

Acting-Sergeant Wm. M'Auley, in reply to Mr. Blake, deposed that he saw Rev. Mr. Eagleton coming from the direction of the brake waving an umbrella over his head, and calling on the party behind him to come on and take the platform. The crowd then rushed over, and a free fight took place. He saw Rev. Mr. Eagleton striking some person on the platform with an umbrella, and he afterwards saw Rev. Mr. Eagleton bleeding.

Mr. James M'Clean, a resident magistrate, on duty during the election, swore that he read the Riot Act, and endeavoured to put an end to the tumult. When he rushed in, they were using sticks and umbrellas all round. He added that Rev. Mr. Eagleton put an old hat on the top of an umbrella and waved it over his head, and shouted, "The hat my father wore." He continued to do this, although witness asked him to restrain himself.

Rev. Mr. Heaney, whose assault upon Colonel Nolan has been described, also joined in the free fight, and fell fighting gloriously for "faith and fatherland."

"We will Crush you when we Get the Power."

An extraordinary speech was delivered on July 29th, 1892, by Rev. Father Behan at an anti-Parnellite meeting in St. Stephen's Green, Dublin. After several attempts to obtain a hearing, the speaker, who was repeatedly interrupted by the Parnellites, reminded them that, nineteen hundred years ago, a man named Herod, whose blasphemous followers declared his voice to be the voice of God, was struck dead. To-day Parnell was constantly flung in their faces. This man, whose memory he detested, had been a curse; but God had thrust him down into the grave, and there his bones were rotting and his flesh putrid. (Loud groans and exclamations.) " I say, you ruffians, I would not have made that statement but for your interruptions." (Further interruptions.) The speaker continued saying the Parnellites were men who did homage to lasciviousness. Every man who liked a loose life, every drunkard, every man who beat his wife—these were Parnellites. Every virtuous man was on the Federation side. Though they might fail in that contest, yet they would win all over the country. The reverend gentleman went on to say, amid loud hisses, "When we are your masters, we will crush you when we get the power." The interruptions continued, and the speaker appealed to his friends near the platform to throw the Parnellites out; but as they did not venture to do so, he said he would call in the police and have them bludgeoned.*

Squeezing Out Subscriptions.

It is manifest, indeed, that the judgments delivered in the Meath election petitions have not had the effect of putting an end to clerical intimidation. Owing to the partial failure of the Evicted Tenants' Fund, the parish priests have in innumerable instances thrown themselves into the work of collecting for the fund, and when they are refused they are not sparing of

* *Daily Express*, July 30th, 1892.

their threats. In a West Cork parish the priest at the conclusion of Mass referred to one of his parishioners —a respectable and well-to-do shopkeeper—as a "low ruffian and a blackguard," because of his refusal to contribute. This shopkeeper is a prominent Parnellite, and he grounded his refusal upon the fact that the money collected was not being impartially administered, and that evicted tenants holding his own political views were denied the relief which had been promised to them, and which they had a right to expect. The priest further asked the congregation to take notice how the man would go into his coffin. He also expressed his astonishment that anybody who had such a shop as that owned by the parishioner in question had declared to oppose his will and to refuse him a subscription.*

Undoubtedly the influence possessed by the priest upon the women of Ireland was used to the utmost. The following letter was received by Mrs. White, of Clara, in the Tullamore Division of King's County, from her parish priest :—

"THE PRESBYTERY, CLARA,
"*July* 24*th*, 1891.

"DEAR MRS. WHITE,—Your name appears in this morning's *Freeman's Journal* among the names of those who graced the Parnellite Convention yesterday by their presence on the balcony. Having appointed you to the high office of president of the Sacred Heart

* *Times*, Jan. 14th, 1893.

Sodality in this parish, I deem it my painful duty to inquire—(1) if this report be correct; and (2), if it is, what course you purpose to pursue in regard of that office. Unless your former high sense of propriety and religion has departed, you must readily perceive the impossibility of maintaining at the head of a religious sodality a lady who could champion Mr. Parnell in the face of all his abominations and in opposition to the solemn condemnation of the Episcopate of the Irish Church. I have hitherto refused, in the absence of any overt act, to believe in your sympathy with the cause of that degraded man, but my duty is now peremptory in the supposition of your presence at the Convention.

"I am faithfully yours,
"MATTHEW GAFFNEY.*

"MRS. P. J. WHITE."

In the Thurles Division, where Mr. Harrison was defeated, Mr. Parnell himself took part in the contest, but to no avail. The *Times* correspondent thus described the scene on August 2nd :—

"The most desperate efforts were made by the clerical party to influence to-day's gathering. Counter-demonstrations were threatened, and Mr. Parnell was warned not to insult his Grace of Cashel by appearing at the palace gates. From the altar, in the streets, and at the homes of the people the clergy gave directions and

* *Freeman's Journal*, July 28th, 1892.

advice, but apparently with little avail, for the people assembled to the extent of some thousands, and cheered Mr. Parnell as heartily as if he were an honoured son of the Church. Some hundreds of *children attending a convent school in the town have, it is stated, by the direction of the priests, for several days knelt in prayer to ask Providence to interpose some obstacle to Mr. Parnell's visit to Thurles."* *

"ARE WE FIT FOR HOME RULE?"

With such scenes occurring in Ireland, is it any wonder that Home Rule is dreaded by the Irish Protestants? Archbishop Croke himself uttered a cry of despair before the general election which is worth remembering and noting to-day. Speaking at Hospital, County Limerick, on May 25th, 1892, he said: "I am greatly afraid that I shall never see a parliament on College Green. I am greatly afraid the cause is lost. Are we really fit for Home Rule, and do we deserve it? Within the last four months I have heard several staunch and intelligent Irishmen say that, considering all that has occurred in our midst since the revelations in the London Divorce Court, and the strange turn that some of the Irish party and a certain section of our people have taken, preferring the interest of one man to the cause of their country, we have given both friends and foes reason to believe that we are at present utterly unfit for Home Rule."

* August 3rd, 1892.

Yes, friends and foes are beginning to see that Home Rule is out of the question. It may perhaps come within "the range of practical politics" in the twentieth century, but now it has receded again into the "dim and distant future."

CHAPTER X.

THE SOUTH MEATH ELECTION, 1892.

THE undue influence of the Irish priest in politics reached its climax in the Meath elections of 1892. "Royal" Meath had for years been noted as a constituency addicted to extreme views and to returning advanced Nationalist members. It was the first constituency represented in Parliament by Mr. Parnell, and he had been preceded in the representation by other Irish parliamentary celebrities. Moreover, the chances of success in County Meath were well balanced. Both the clerical party and the Parnellite party had a large following, and it was evident that whichever side won would achieve a great moral victory. The candidates for South Meath were Mr. Fullam, the nominee of the priest, a gentleman hitherto absolutely unknown to fame, and Mr. J. J. Dalton, formerly member for West Donegal, and a returned Australian. The candidates for North Meath were Mr. Davitt (Anti-Parnellite) and Mr. Pierce Mahony (Parnellite).

A Clerical Caucus.

The campaign against the Parnellite candidates commenced on June 1st, 1892, when a convention was held in Trim to adopt clerical candidates. The laity attended, but only to receive orders. The prominent part of the organisation fell to the superior station, influence, ability, antecedents, and traditions of the priesthood. From the first moment the clergy threw themselves into the contest with all the overwhelming power, organisation, and discipline of their order, and with the zeal of men who could be reckoned upon to have no fear from popular insult or violence. These are the very words of Judge O'Brien in his judgment on the election petition in which he described the political action of the priesthood of his own denomination. "The Church," he went on, "became converted for the time being into a vast political agency, a great moral machine, moving with resistless influence, united action, and single will. Every priest was a canvasser; the canvass was everywhere—on the altar, in the vestry, on the roads, in the houses. There was no place left for evasion, excuse, affected ignorance, weakness, or treachery. Of the ten polling-places, there was but one in which there was not a priest as agent and personation agent, with or without laymen. . . . At the counting of the votes there were seven priests named to attend on behalf of Mr. Fullam, with but one layman. Whether or not their presence on such an occasion could have any influence, Mr. Fullam had certainly at least a staff of expert and trained logicians, who were more than a match for his opponent on the many questions that arise over voting-papers, and which are of such moment in case of a narrow majority."

THE CAMPAIGN AGAINST INDEPENDENT POLITICAL OPINION.

Such was Mr. Fullam's highly equipped army of agents, of whom, indeed, the Judge remarked that they appeared to have fulfilled the positions of principals, while the candidate was merely their agent.

It next remains to be seen how this army conducted its campaign. The first and gravest grounds on which the validity of the election was questioned was the celebrated pastoral letter of the Most Rev. Dr. Nulty, which was read in all the churches of the County Meath on July 3rd, 1892. This document was the mainspring, the motor muscle of the whole ecclesiastical organisation in the diocese. It set forth, to use Judge O'Brien's words, "the Divine authority of the Church, the obligations of the moral law which Mr. Parnell had violated, and the responsibility of those who supported Parnellism,—all alike with great power of expression and moral dignity and severity calculated to have the most powerful effect on the community to which it was addressed. Parnellism was alleged to strike at the root and sap the very foundations of the Catholic faith. It was stated to have been declared unlawful and unholy by the successors of the Apostles, though the resolution of the bishops, which was the foundation of this proposition, related solely to the question of political leadership. Those who refused to accept that proposition on the assumed authority of the Catholic Hierarchy were pronounced to have deprived themselves of every reason for believing in the doctrines of a revealed religion, which all rested upon the same authority. Invincible ignorance, that exception which identifies the condemned doctrine with heresy, was allowed possibly to excuse misguided men and women, for it was laid down authoritatively that no intelligent or well-informed person could remain a Catholic and continue to cling to Parnellism."

THE BISHOP'S THUNDER.

"The bishop preached twice on June 29th in Trim. In one discourse, according to the evidence, he alluded to the crisis in the coming election, and said that Parnellism was nothing but a heresy, and that he would approach the death-bed of the heretic and the profligate with greater confidence as to his salvation than that of a Parnellite, and he added an expression which, in the silence of the printed reports, I would not," said Judge O'Brien, "have trusted my own note to quote until after comparing it with the official report, in reference to women who sympathise with Parnellism. In the other discourse on the same day he said that Parnellism was moral ruin, that it was improper and unholy, that Parnellites were losing the faith and becoming heretics; he also declared, following the same line as the pastoral, if the people did not believe him on the doctrine of Parnellism, how could they believe him on such questions as Confession and Communion?"

"The Shadow of Sin."

Such was the line of attack inaugurated by the bishop of the diocese. The leading idea was that the particular form of political opinion known as Parnellism was sinful, and that it was a matter of eternal damnation or salvation which was in question. The priesthood developed the idea with fidelity and distinctness—carried it out and demonstrated it in every possible way. "The shadow of sin was over the whole contest"—as the judge declared in the summing up of the effect of the bishop's pastoral letter. The pulpit and the altar were used everywhere as a means of spiritual intimidation. "In no other place on the earth," said one of the Roman Catholic counsel for the petitioner, "in Pagan or Christian times, was there anything resembling or approaching the power and influence which a Catholic priest standing on the altar had, and he should shrink from abusing it." Such considerations never weighed for one moment with the Meath priesthood. On the contrary, many of them, using the influence of and backed by the altar, using the presence of the Host and the administration of the Sacrament, adjured their congregations to vote for Fullam. What humble Catholic Irishman could withstand such powerful, tremendous, supernatural influence? "I think," said counsel, "it is more powerful during the Mass, and a more illegitimate exercise of such influence than if it were spoken at Vespers or at any other service, and that it is more effective when delivered from the altar than from the pulpit. It is perhaps only the Catholic who can comprehend the sanctity that surrounds the priest when celebrating the 'awful sacrifice of Mass,' and who has just given Communion to the people. It is irresistible to simple, trusting, and believing minds."

Space precludes the possibility of going at any length into the evidence which was given to show the utterly outrageous conduct of the priests in these Meath elections. All that is necessary is to give an outline of the manner in which the campaign determined upon by the bishop was carried out by his clergy. No attempt will be made to dress up the facts with rhetorical embellishment. They are given simply as they were sworn to in the witness-box.

"FIRE TO THEIR TOES AND HEELS."

Father O'Connell delivered a sermon about which several witnesses gave evidence. After saying that he would meet those of his congregation who would not go to one of Mr. Fullam's meetings "on the road, at their houses, outside the chapel, and at the rails, and put fire to their toes and heels," he made some remark about the Parnellites going to the altar and committing sacrilege, called them anti-Catholics and heretics, said their conduct was savagery, and added that he had never yet been put down, and he would not be put down now.

A Sin to be a Parnellite.

John Rogers, of Piercetown, deposed that on June 29th he heard Father Fitzsimmons preach at Ardhill Castle, Mr. Dalton, the petitioner, being present. The preacher took for his text, "Thou art Peter, and upon this rock will I build My Church," and went on to say that the enemy was amongst them. He then said something about private judgment, and that the Church had survived attacks from without, and would survive the attacks from within. Subsequently he met Father Davis, who said he was a Parnellite, and that he would have to give it up. Witness asked him was it a sin to be a Parnellite, and Father Davis said it was, and that if he did not follow the bishop in that matter he could not follow him in anything else.

"In the Name of God."

Richard Macintosh stated that on the Sunday before the election, at Ardcath, Father Carey, during Mass, produced a ballot-paper, and asked the people "In the name of God to put the cross opposite the name of Fullam."

The Right of the Church.

Robert J. Heany, of Duleek, deposed to having had a conversation about the election with Father Guillick, who said that, according to Dr. Reilly's book, the

Church had a right to ask the people to vote on certain occasions in a certain way.

CLERICAL OBSTRUCTION AT THE POLL.

Anthony Grogan, of Longwood, gave evidence of being deprived of his vote. Father Shaw was in the polling-booth when he came up to vote. As the name on the register was Anthony Geoghegan, Father Shaw objected to his being allowed to vote, and witness went away. He returned twice subsequently, and on the last occasion, which was about half-past seven, he was asked to take an oath that he was the person described in the register. He consented to do so; but Father Shaw had a conversation with the presiding officer, and he was kept there till after the poll was closed.

A GROUP OF STARTLING UTTERANCES.

Patrick Byrne stated that Father Fay said he would treat the Parnellites like beasts in the Zoological Gardens. He also called them followers of Garibaldi. Thomas Dorby stated that he told Father M'Donnell he should vote for Dalton, and the priest said he would go to hell.

Christopher Brogan deposed that the chapel gates were closed against Parnellites during Mass at Clonard on July 10th. The witness asked Sheridan, who had charge of the gate, what they had done to be kept out of Mass, and he was told to go to Roper, the Protestant clergyman. He tried to get in a second time, but was refused. On the previous Sunday he heard Rev. Michael Woods read the bishop's pastoral.

Thomas Murray, a farmer, heard Father Richard M'Donnell preach at Kill Chapel on July 3rd. After having read the pastoral, the preacher described the witness and others who had canvassed for Mr. Dalton as disreputable individuals, and that it would be worse for them here and hereafter. He advised the congregation to go to the meeting at Longwood and to bring blackthorn sticks, and said that he himself would bring one to defend himself.

Thomas Connor swore that Father Callery at Rathfiegh Chapel referred to those who would go to a Parnellite meeting at Tara as adulterers.

Thomas M'Ivor and James Bennett deposed that before the election Father Carey, during Mass, asked the congregation "for God's sake to make their cross after the name of Fullam."

John Fry, of Moynalty, stated that on the Sunday before the election Father Kelly, during a sermon, said the question was a religious one, and he hoped that the people would go with their bishop. After the declaration of the poll the witness was burnt in effigy.

Michael Gaughran heard Father M'Donnell say during Mass that the time had come when nobody could remain a Catholic and be a Parnellite. Turning round, the priest struck the altar and said he knew who would be marked men.

Thomas Byrne, farmer and shopkeeper, deposed that since the election he had heard Father Brady preach and say that he did not see how those who were "going against him" or "maligning him" could expect him to visit them or administer the Sacraments to them.

Peter Magrath, a reporter, deposed that at a Federation meeting in Drogheda the respondent thanked the priests for the fight which they had made for him.

A Scene at a Death-bed.

John Murtagh, who appeared in the witness-box with a bandaged hand, stated that he went to Father Fagan in Kildalkey to ask him to attend a sick woman at his house. The priest asked him if he had a vote, and witness said he did not know until he looked after it. Father Fagan then asked him, if he had a vote, to whom would he give it. He also said that Parnell was a blackguard, and ridiculed him. The witness said they knew now who were their friends and who were their enemies, and the priest then said, "May the landlords come and hunt you all to hell's blazes out of the country." The witness said, "You are kind to your neighbours." Father Fagan told him he was a blackguard and a ruffian, and that he would kick him into the ditch. "I told him," said witness, "that I would kick him like a dog if he raised his arm to me." Father Fagan called him a ruffian, and said that the witness would want him on the Last Day, adding,

"I won't hear the woman's confession." The witness replied, "I don't care whether you do or not; I will go to Father Martin, the parish priest." The witness walked away. His wife was then dead.

CANVASSING IN THE CONFESSIONAL BOX.

William Sherry said he was canvassed in the confessional by Father Behan, who told him to vote for Mr. Fullam, and that he might shout for Dalton in the streets if he liked. James Cowley and George Plunket also gave evidence of being canvassed by the same priest in the confessional. A man named Nowling deposed to hearing Father Behan say, during Mass, that those who interfered with the priests frequently died without the priest.

PRIESTS AS PERSONATION AGENTS.

At Clonard Father M'Donnell was standing so close to the ballot-box that witness complained to the presiding officer. Father M'Donnell said he would stand where he liked. At Longwood two of witness's personation agents were refused admission by Rev. Mr. Shaw, who was inside, and were not allowed to enter till witness came up. At Balrivor, where Rev. Patrick Fagan was acting as personation agent for Mr. Fullam, at Athboy, and at Trim, the booths were occupied by priests as personation agents. At the nomination Mr. Fullam was attended by eight or ten clergymen and one layman.

Bernard Carew, a brother of the ex-member for Kildare, deposed that at Summerhill polling-station he was spat upon by the crowd. Father Buchanan was with the crowd, and Father Fay was also with them, but neither interfered to protect him. Outside there was a meeting, at which he was attacked by Mr. Fullam and Father Cantwell, the latter of whom denounced him for leaving the Church during the reading of the "beautiful pastoral." The crowd then rushed at him and called him names.

Michael Murtagh deposed to having been present when Father M'Donnell canvassed a man named Darly, to whom he said, "Are you a Catholic, or do you want to go to hell?" Father M'Donnell then canvassed witness, who replied that he would vote for Mr. Dalton. Thereupon Father M'Donnell said, "You seem to be as satisfied to go to the devil as to go to heaven."

These were the methods by which the elections of North and South Meath were won for Mr. Gladstone. But even when victory sat triumphant on the banners of Clerical Coercion the priests were not satisfied.

How the Petition was Treated.

When the political party against whom all these electoral malpractices had been put in force determined to petition against the return of the bishop's nominee, the most virtuous indignation was assumed by the priesthood. One notorious priest, Father John Fay, of Summerhill, while the petition was pending, dealt with it in a sermon on November 6th. In the course of his remarks he said :—

"Before I have an opportunity of meeting you again, I shall be on my trial at Trim with the other priests of the diocese and the bishop, and I am glad of the opportunity of showing up the character of these men who will give evidence against me. We will expose again the scandal of the Divorce Court. These people, imbued with the devil, will pursue me to the end. I expect that I am prepared for it. I tell you the devil will attack me, and they are possessed by the devil of impurity, the most frightful of passions. Now, this is pure Parnellism. Is it not a glorious thing to put our bishop like a common criminal in the box after twenty-nine years of service and toil and devotion for you? Now, report this, every word, accurately, and put it in your *Independent*. Don't leave out a single word, for I'll be there, and I'll prove that every witness that will come up against me is a black-dyed scamp. I never intimidated you. I never said I would kill you or break your neck, or said you would go to hell. You may go there if you like. We will resume this in Trim." The reverend father proceeded to lecture on the due preparation for Extreme Unction, and said : "You may think it strange for me to refer to bodily cleanliness, but I find it necessary from my great experience; but I suppose they will put an end to me on the petition in Trim next week." Then he said that "they should not look upon him as a mere man : if they did, they might have some prejudice against him, for all had their shortcomings. The priest is the ambassador of Jesus Christ, and not like other ambassadors. They carried their Lord and Master about with them, and when the priest was with the people the Almighty God was with them."

ATTACHMENT OF FATHER FAY.

It would be hard to imagine anything more flagrantly in contempt of court than such a tirade, or one more manifestly uttered for the purpose of intimidating witnesses in the forthcoming trial. Accordingly, on November 11th, 1892, an application was made in Dublin for the attachment of Father Fay, and the Court granted the motion in a unanimous judgment. The Lord Chief Justice of Ireland, in pronouncing sentence of a month's imprisonment, said :—

"He is an educated gentleman. Is his education any alleviation? His education ought to have taught him that he should not have done this. Is there any mitigation to be found in the priestly character? The mission of the priest and the Christian clergyman is to proclaim and to enforce by precept and example the gospel of peace. I will not refer again to these words, or indicate again in express language the doom which is indicated for those who would oppose him. The time was the Sabbath, the place was the church—even on the altar. I stop—I refrain from comment, because I do not wish to harrow the feelings of the reverend gentleman. I wish I could find any mitigation of this language."

WHITEWASHING THE CLERICAL CULPRIT.

On his release from jail Father Fay was met at Maynooth by a number of Roman Catholic clergy, including Dr. O'Donnell, the Bishop of Raphoe, when an address of sympathy was presented. The incident is worth noting, as clearly proving the feeling of the Irish Roman Catholic Hierarchy was entirely with Father Fay, and that his incriminating language was quite justifiable. And yet it has been demonstrated that in no electoral struggle of the present century had Irish priests sunk so low in their efforts to drive their parishioners to the polls. The clutch which the Roman Catholic Hierarchy has upon the ignorance and credulity of the Irish people has at last been well shown by the evidence in the Meath petitions, and it is plain that the Irish voter can be and is swayed to a terrible extent by threats and promises of future punishment pronounced by his priest. The counsel for the petitioner put the case strongly enough in commenting on the pastoral of the bishop.

A COMPARISON WITH ENGLISH CLERGY.

"What," he said, "would be the position of this country, what would be the position of England, what would be the position of all free institutions, if any ecclesiastic—say the Archbishop of Canterbury—

dealing with some of the many isms that are now returned to the Imperial Parliament- socialism, labourism, or any of these isms take the doctrine of socialism, that so many of these labour candidates hold—writing to the electors of the district in a pastoral, should say : ' You will cease to remain good Protestants ; you will cease to be members of the Establishment, if you give your adhesion to any candidate of socialistic views, because these views are plainly a violation of the commandment, " Thou shalt not steal ; thou shalt not covet thy neighbour's goods " ? ' If such addresses to any faith of any colour were suffered so to invade the constitutional right of any elector to exercise his free franchise, where would be the freedom of citizenship ? "

Destruction of Civil Liberty.

The answer is plain. There would be no civil liberty left if such a state of affairs could be tolerated. And yet exactly such a state of affairs has been proved to be found existing in Ireland. The judgment of election judges in South Meath shows that voters were debarred from the exercise of their political judgment by the whole corporate Roman Catholic clergy of the district. It was made a matter of eternal salvation to vote in one particular way. The Church of Rome became, for the time being, a huge political and moral machine, moving, as the judge expressed it, with " its resistless influence and united action." What wonder, indeed, that Mr. Fullam was elected and that Mr.

Gladstone's allies in other constituencies in Ireland were unduly elected by the spiritual corruption and moral coercion of the priesthood! The wonder is that there were found so many to poll for an Independent candidate.

After the election was declared void, the *Lyceum* (January number, 1893), a monthly periodical, which is the intellectual organ of the Dublin clericals, and is published under the sanction and revision of the hierarchy, spoke quite plainly upon the claims of the clergy to dictate political opinion. It said:—

"To give a more apposite example, suppose that a parliamentary candidate presented himself in Meath with the programme of Cavour, . . . would Mr. Justice O'Brien still maintain that 'no question of moral obligation' for the voters would arise, and that 'the conduct of a voter' who helped them by his votes would not be a sin?"

And again:—

"We have shown, further, that the exercise of the franchise in Meath, as elsewhere, may involve grave moral obligations—obligations under sin, even mortal sin; that it may in certain cases be mortally sinful to vote for or against particular parliamentary candidates, and that when such a case occurs it may be the duty of a confessor to intimate his obligation to a penitent, and deny him sacramental absolution should he refuse to comply with it."

THE SHADOW OF SACERDOTALISM.

How often have the Liberal party scoffed at the idea of clerical oppression and priestly interference in Ireland! The grave and serious facts of the Meath petition have dispersed all doubt in the matter. It is not a bogey raised by Unionists and Irish Protestants.

What the fate of Ireland would be when handed over to the political supremacy of such a faction as elected Mr. Fullam may be imagined. *The shadow of sacerdotalism* is over the Irish constituencies, and it is to the solid results of that sacerdotalism, as evidenced by the Meath case, that Mr. Gladstone now holds his present position in Parliament. This is a matter which comes home to the heart and conscience of every Protestant in England and Scotland. It is time the matter was looked into. The people of England must be asked if clerical parties in politics are to be tolerated. As Sir Henry James once remarked: " Every foreign land that has ever endured the existence and influence of a clerical party has suffered in its freedom. Liberties have been lost and progress has been delayed by the influence of sacerdotalism in politics." Is it surprising that the Irish Protestants are determined to make any sacrifice to avert a system of Home Rule which will establish that influence and endow it with complete parliamentary power over their lives and properties?

CHAPTER XI.

THE NORTH MEATH ELECTION.

THE North Meath election was conducted on behalf of Mr. Michael Davitt, the clerical nominee, in precisely the same manner as that in the Southern Division. The only difference was that the procedure was more violent, and that the clergy themselves indulged their ardour to the extent of using physical force. Mr. Pierce Mahony, who formerly represented the constituency in Parliament, is a Protestant, and Mr. Davitt endeavoured during his canvass to lay upon his antagonist the brand of being the son of a "Souper," a term of opprobrium well known in Ireland for a proselytising Protestant. Mr. Davitt placed himself and left himself entirely in the hands of the clergy to manage and procure his election. The "Father of the Land League," and the quondam member of the Supreme Council of the Irish Republican Brotherhood, suddenly became the obedient child of the Church. On his arrival in the constituency he immediately repaired to the residence of Bishop Nulty. Thence he proceeded to and returned from the Convention in the Catholic Seminary, where he was adopted candidate.

From the hands of a priest, one of the treasurers of the fund raised by the organising committee for election expenses, he received £200 to pay the sheriff's expenses. Priests accompanied and attended him everywhere, canvassed for him, delivered addresses from the altars and sermons from the pulpits on his behalf. He lived with a priest during all his stay in the constituency, and gave his residence as a priest's house in the appointment of his personation agents. He took the services of the priests, and went to the poll on the nomination of the bishop, whose pastoral letter was promulgated on his behalf in every parish in the division. There cannot be the smallest doubt in the world that Mr. Davitt was nominated member for North Meath by the Church of Rome acting as a political organisation, and that his election was a fraud upon the constitutional rights of every voter in the division.

It would be only a task of repetition to go into detail as to the scenes and episodes which took place in this election. The distinctive feature, however, of personal violence upon the part of the priesthood must be exhibited in all its scandalous brutality. On July 10th Bishop Nulty addressed his congregation in Navan upon the subject of the election, and used language which was certainly interpreted, if not meant, as an invitation to Mr. Davitt's party to use physical force in order to win their battle. Mr. James Lawlor, town clerk of Navan, gave evidence as follows :—

Bishop Nulty's Sermon.

"I was at Mass at Navan on July 10th. Rev. Dr. Nulty spoke after the first Gospel. He said that Mr. Davitt and his supporters were coming to Navan, and he said he was coming there more in the interests of religion than in a political matter. He said he was coming in the interests of religion. He said this was more a religious than a political question. He said that the number that would come would cow the Parnellites, and that the Parnellites were cowards and rowdies. I left the chapel at that stage, and know nothing further."

Bernard Clarke said: "I heard Father McNamee read the pastoral at Navan on July 3rd. He said there would be an important sermon at last Mass, which I attended. Rev. Dr. Nulty, the bishop, preached the promised sermon."

"What did the bishop say?"

"He said there was to be a meeting of Mr. Davitt's supporters; that Mr. Davitt would be there himself on the following Sunday; to come in like lambs and go out like lambs, but to be armed with sticks, and if booed or insulted that the people would get their skulls broke in, and that they would be beaten with sticks."

"Is that all you remember?"

"I left the chapel when I heard him say we would get our skulls broke in."

FATHER DUFFY'S STICK.

The priests were as good as the bishop's word, as the sworn evidence proves.

James Gannon, of Rodenstown, said: "I attended Mass early in June. Father Duffy, the curate, addressed the people before the last Gospel. He said 'there was a meeting got up in Syddon for that day, got up against the priests and against the Church, and he advised none of his people to attend it, and not to be seen with such a motley crew or crowd; that their real object in organising it was to sell their porter.' That might be a reference to myself, as I was engaged in the spirit trade and I helped to organise the meeting.

"On July 10th I attended a meeting at Navan. Father Duffy was in Navan also. He came home before me. About eight o'clock I was in the street with some friends. Father Duffy came down from the parochial house with a stick in his hand; he was walking in a defiant manner. When the people saw him in the middle of the road, they divided to allow him to pass. He turned back after passing through the crowd, and he asked me what I was doing—why didn't I go home? I said the people were doing no harm. He told them to go home in a stern kind of way."

After some conversation, in which Father Duffy threatened to do his best to get the witness's licence suspended, the crowd called for a cheer for Mahony. Then, according to Gannon, "He raised a stick and struck one of the men in the crowd. He struck him on the head, which was cut and bleeding. Meehul, the man struck, had said or done nothing to Father Duffy. He then struck another man named Donegan, raising a lump on his temple. The people then rushed in and took hold of the stick. I told them to have patience. I got into the crowd and pushed them on one side. I asked Father Duffy to leave go the stick. I said, 'As bad as you think the people, you'll not be hit. You have nothing to be afraid of.' The people then let go the stick."

There was no provocation of any sort given.

Thomas Meade said he was on the street at Rodenstown on the evening of the nomination. "I remember Father Duffy coming up. He struck me on the outside of the eye with a big stick he had. It drew my blood. I gave him no offence, nor said a word. He struck another man also."

Francis Doorigan said: "I remember Father Duffy coming down the street of Loganstown on July 10th. He struck me on the head with a stick. I was standing with my back to the side of a car. I did not say anything, or offer any offence to the reverend gentleman, before he struck."

FATHER CLARKE KNOCKS DOWN AN OLD MAN.

A grosser case of unprovoked brutality upon the part of a priest occurred on the polling day of the worth Meath election. Anthony Smith said he was at Nobber on the day of polling. He saw Owen Reilly knocked down by Father Clarke. " I was a few yards from Reilly; he was addressing some remarks, but to no one in particular. Reilly said that every one should be allowed to vote according to his conscience; then Father Clarke said, 'Withdraw those words,' and I turned for an instant, and when I looked round Reilly was on the ground, and appeared insensible. He was muttering something like a man in a dream. Mr. Mahony then appeared on the scene and asked the people to be quiet, and they took his bidding."

Mr. Pierce Mahony, the petitioner, in his evidence stated:—

"On the day of the polling I went to Nobber, and was met at the station by a few friends, and the sergeant of police, who communicated to me that he hadn't sufficient force to protect me, and he asked me not to go up. I told him I must visit the booths."

"Do you remember being in one of the booths when some one called for you?" "Yes: Mr. O'Brien."

"When you went out, did you see a priest, whose name you since learned to be Father Clarke, on the roadway?"—"I saw him surrounded by a very excited crowd. I rushed into the middle, and tried to push them back. I inquired what happened, and was told that a man had been knocked down by a priest. I went over to the man. He was just beginning, apparently, to become conscious, and I heard a little more about it. I then went back to the priest, and

I said, 'You know that no man in this country likes to hit a gentleman of your cloth, and under the circumstances it is a cowardly thing to hit any man.' He said, 'If you don't withdraw that I'll hit you.' I said, 'I'll not withdraw it. It was a cowardly thing.' The crowd then closed in. Then a reverend gentleman, whom I since learned was Father Everard, came out of another booth and took Father Clarke away. Mr. Bennett Burleigh (of the London *Telegraph*) drew my attention to the fact that a magistrate named Mr. Walker was on the street. I went up and asked him was he a magistrate? He said he was. I called his attention to the fact that a very serious assault had been committed, and I expressed the opinion that Father Clarke ought to be arrested. He then said it would be—I think the word he used was dangerous—to arrest a clergyman. Mr. Burleigh said, 'I don't know what you do in this country, but we would make short work of him in England.' I said I thought it would be his duty to see that the police had his proper name and address, in order that he might be prosecuted."

It is almost pathetic to see in all the evidence the innate respect and reverence which the Irish voters could not help showing to their priest, even under the contumely of insult and violence. The awe and obedience which the majority of the voters displayed is well described by Mr. Patrick Kelsh, who acted as personation agent to Mr. Mahony. He described in his evidence how an illiterate voter came into the polling-booth and threw himself down on his knees before a priest, Father Cassidy, and in a faltering voice said, "I will vote for Mr. Davitt." "He threw himself down on his knees as if he was going to confession,"—such was the expression of the witness.

Father Brady's Sweet Reasonableness.

James Daly swore that on the second day before the polling he met Father Brady. "He asked me was I a Davittite or a Mahonyite. I said I believed in the policy of Independent Opposition. On that he jumped off the car and caught me by the throat, and dragged me about on the road. He held a whip over my head. I begged him for God's sake not to strike me—that I was a good Catholic, and that I had never insulted a clergyman in my life, or never meant to do so. Then he gave me a final shake and let me go. I did not forget that he was a priest, and was carrying the Blessed Sacrament about with him, and on that account I did not or would not insult him."

Men, women, and children were all fair game to the militant priests in North Meath.

Knocking Down Children.

Patrick Sherlock deposed:—"On July 10th, the day of the meeting at Navan, a procession came in led by Mr. Davitt. There were thirty or forty clergymen present. I was standing on the Court-house steps, and there was a girl standing just opposite me, and a horse was running away behind; and as the horse was running away, Mr. Davitt and the priests turned, and as they were turned back they met the girl just opposite me, and the clergyman up with his umbrella and knocked her hat off with the left hand, and struck her with the stick with the right hand."

"Was she speaking or cheering?"—"No more than I was."

"Did he knock her down?"—"He did; and there was another priest coming to hit her, and she lying."

"Do you say that he was going again to hit her?"—"Yes; and I lifted her up. I said he was not a clergyman that could strike a girl. He said that 'he would put his stick down my throat if I interfered.'"

"Was not the girl bleeding?"—"She had on a white dress, and there was blood running down from her head."

"As far as you saw on that occasion, were not the clergymen the ringleaders of the mob?"—"There was nothing going in with Mr. Davitt on that day but murderers."

These are only a few facts which came out in evidence at the North Meath trial, and they may safely be left without comment to the consideration of the lovers of civil and religious freedom.

CHAPTER XII.

MR. GLADSTONE ON PRIESTS IN POLITICS.

THE one great predominating and intractable fact which stands out clearly crystallised from the mass of evidence which has been adduced in these pages is the claim of the Roman Catholic Hierarchy and priesthood of Ireland to stand above the law. If this monstrous claim has been made in the face of an Imperial Parliament sitting in London, what claims may we not live to see when or if the Roman Catholic Hierarchy practically nominate and elect an Irish Parliament, principally Roman Catholic, in Dublin? What civil allegiance would or could such an assembly demand of Cardinal Logue or Archbishop Walsh? and would not these prelates repudiate such a demand under certain conditions and circumstances? Do not all the burning questions arise with tenfold force, which Mr. Gladstone discussed with such eager acrimony in 1874 in his pamphlets, *The Vatican Decrees in their Bearing on Civil Allegiance,* and *Vaticanism?* It certainly seems so. In any case the elucidation of these questions may, perhaps, be assisted by referring to Mr. Gladstone's own words upon the subject.*

"A Policy of Violence."

Mr. Gladstone was called to account for the following passage in an article from his pen. He said it was impossible to Romanise England " when Rome has substituted for the proud boast of *semper eadem* a policy of violence and change in faith; when she has refurbished and paraded anew every rusty tool she was fondly thought to have disused ; when no one can become her convert without renouncing his moral and mental freedom, and placing his civil loyalty and duty at the mercy of another; and when she has equally repudiated modern thought and ancient history."

With all the evidence of the Meath petitions fresh in our recollections, may we not say with Mr. Gladstone to our Roman Catholic fellow-subjects, that "the people of this country who fully believe in their loyalty are entitled on purely civil grounds to expect from them some declaration or manifestation of opinion in reply to that ecclesiastical party in their Church who have laid down in their name principles adverse to the purity and integrity of civil allegiance " ? Mr. Gladstone gave deep offence in 1874 by his plain speaking.

---

* *The Vatican Decrees in their Bearing on Civil Allegiance: a Political Expostulation.* 1874.
Vaticanism :—an Answer to Replies and Reproofs. By Right Hon. W. E. Gladstone, M.P. John Murray. 1875.

He has withdrawn nothing save the imputation upon the civil loyalty of Roman Catholic converts. His original pamphlet was treated as an attack made upon Roman Catholics, and as an insult offered to them. The same may be said again. What was his answer? "If," he replied, "I am told that he who animadverts upon these assails thereby, or insults, Roman Catholics at large, who do not choose their ecclesiastical rulers, and can and are not recognised as having any voice in the government of their Church, I cannot be bound by or accept a proposition which seems to me so little in accordance with reason." Mr. Gladstone's defence against the attacks of controversialists of 1874 holds equally good to-day. Any language, indeed, which has been used in these pages in criticism of the political attitude of the Church of Rome, compared with the language of the present Prime Minister in 1874 is as "moonlight is to sunlight and as water is to wine.' Nor has one word been said as to the doctrinal or theological belief of the Roman Catholic Church. The whole grievance lies in charges of a civil and political character.

"VOLLEYS OF SPIRITUAL CENSURES."

It may not be amiss to recall some of Mr. Gladstone's views, culling only a few flowers of rhetoric from the wreath which he laid at the feet of the Pope. Here is a description of the Church of Rome, for instance followed by an opinion as startling and extreme :—

"A religious society which delivers volleys of spiritual censures in order to impede the performance of civil duties does all for mischief that is in its power to do, and brings into question, in the face of the State, its title to civil protection." It would be interesting to know how Mr. Gladstone felt when he read Bishop Nulty's pastoral in the Meath election.

Again we have quoted the repugnance of the Roman Catholic priests in Meath to "pure Protestantism." What does Mr. Gladstone say on this point? "The manful Protestantism of mediæval times had its activity almost entirely in the sphere of public, national, and State rights. Too much attention, in my opinion, cannot be fastened on this point. It is the very root and kernel of the matter. Individual servitude, however abject, will not satisfy the party now dominant in the Latin Church. The State must also be a slave." This is precisely the attitude of the Irish Protestants. They say theirs is a public and national and a State right—a right to remain under the authority of the Parliament of the United Kingdom, a right to remain citizens of equal degree with their brethren in Great Britain, a right not to be governed by an external and foreign Power such as Mr. Gladstone himself described so fully and effectually. Home Rule granted, therefore, Mr. Gladstone has kindly demonstrated that the State in Ireland would be the slave of the Roman Catholic Church. Mr. Redmond and his handful of followers might resist, but how will they be met?

"A Daring Raid."

Archbishop Croke during the general election stated to one of his clergy, Rev. Dr. White, of Kilrush, County Clare, "that he had entered into communication with all the Roman Catholic bishops in the world, and that when the proper time came they would be prepared to oppose the Parnellite pretensions, and also to provide funds for sustaining the Irish cause."*

The terms of Archbishop Croke's letter to his foreign brethren would be an interesting study. We may rest assured it will never see the light. It remains, however, on record, that an Irish prelate is prepared to go any length under an Imperial Parliament to crush a political opponent. What will he not do under a Roman Catholic Parliament? Will he not dare to follow in the steps of the Pontiff and condemn (in Mr. Gladstone's own words) "free speech, free writing, a free press, toleration of Nonconformity, liberty of conscience, the study of civil and philosophical matters in independence of the ecclesiastical authority, marriage unless sacramentally contracted, and the definition of the state of the civil rights (*jura*) of the Church"? and will he not demand for the Church "the title to define its own civil rights, together with a Divine right to use physical force"? Each and every one of these contentions has been made by the Church of Rome in Ireland during the past eight years. Ulster agrees with Mr.

* *Weekly National Press*, June 20th, 1892.

Gladstone's solemn asseveration in the *Vatican Decrees*: " It must be for some political object of a very tangible kind that the risks of so daring a raid upon the civil sphere have been deliberately run."

In the case of Ireland undoubtedly the direct object of the claims of sacerdotalism which have been set forth is to assist a political party to gain what is called Home Rule.

The Intrusion of Rome into Civil Affairs.

The Protestants object to Home Rule on many grounds, but largely because of the political power of the Roman Catholic Church and the manner in which it has been used. "As a rule," said Mr. Gladstone in *Vaticanism*, "the real independence of states and nations depends upon the exclusion of foreign influence proper from their civil affairs. Wherever the spirit of freedom, even if ever so faintly, breathes, it resents and reacts against any intrusion of another people or power into the circle of interior concerns as alike dangerous and disgraceful." In Ireland no man can again deny that the Church of Rome has intruded itself into the circle of its interior concerns. And the Irish Protestants can find no better words to describe their objections to the disagreeable distinction of that Church than those of Mr. Gladstone himself. "She alone," he said in *Vaticanism*, "arrogates to herself the right to speak to the State, not as a subject, but as a superior; not as pleading the right of conscience staggered by the fear of sin, but as a vast incorporation, setting up a rival law against the State in the State's own domain, and claiming for it, with a higher sanction, the title to similar coercive means of enforcement." Again: "To secure rights has been and is the aim of the Christian civilisation; to destroy them, and to establish the resistless, domineering action of a purely central power, is the aim of the Roman policy."

Mr. Gladstone's Description of the Organisation of Papal Power.

Mr. Gladstone has described the working of the machine which has given him so curious a majority for Home Rule: "We see before us the Pope, the bishops, the priesthood, and the people. The priests are absolute over the people, the bishops over both, the Pope over all. Each inferior may appeal against his superior; but he appeals to a tribunal which is irresponsible, which he has no share, direct or indirect, in controlling, and which during all the long centuries of its existence, but especially during the latest of them, has had for its cardinal rule this—that all its judgments should be given in the sense most calculated to build up priestly power as against the people, episcopal power as against the priests, Papal power against all three."

These outbursts of indignant remonstrance and denunciation from Mr. Gladstone were all called forth by the action of the Roman Catholic Hierarchy in procuring the rejection in 1873 of his Irish University Bill by "the direct influence which they exercised over a certain number of Irish members of Parliament."* The Irish Protestants quote them now with tenfold force to express these views upon a tremendous constitutional change in the Government of the country. We say in the light of all past experience that, given a Home Rule Parliament, there would be no law in Ireland; for law cannot exist whenever a body of men like the Roman Catholic Hierarchy claim and exercise a power of annulling or a power of dispensing with the law.

* Mr. Gladstone's words are worth quoting as a contribution to the irony of history: "When Parliament had passed the Church Act of 1869 and the Land Act of 1870 there remained only, under the great head of Imperial equity, one serious question to be dealt with—that of the Higher Education. I consider that the Liberal majority in the House of Commons, and the Government to which I had the honour and satisfaction to belong, formally tendered payment in full of this portion of the debt by the Irish University Bill of Feb. 1873. Some, indeed, think it was overpaid: a question into which this is manifestly not the place to enter. But the Roman Catholic prelacy of Ireland thought fit to procure the rejection of that measure by the direct influence which they exercised over a certain number of Irish members of Parliament, and by the temptation which they thus offered, the bid, in effect, which (to use a homely phrase) they made to attract the support of the Tory Opposition. Their efforts were crowned with a complete success. From that time forward I have felt that the situation was changed, and that important matter would have to be cleared by suitable explanations. The debt to Ireland had been paid: a debt to the country at large had still to be disposed of, and this has come to be the duty of the hour."—*Vatican Decrees*, pp. 59, 60.

"ABSOLUTISM."

"This exemption of the individual," says Mr. Gladstone, "be he who he may, from the restraints of the law is the very thing that in England we term absolutism. By absolutism we mean the superiority of a personal will to law, for the purpose of putting aside or changing law." What Ulster says, speaking in the name of Irish Protestantism, is that an Irish Parliament would be merely the tool of the majority, which would be the nominees of the Roman Catholic Church. It would be the apotheosis of the priest in politics.

The strongest and most convincing arguments against such a monstrous arrangement are to be found in Mr. Gladstone's own writings.

Can he explain himself away?

"ADVERSE TO FREEDOM IN THE STATE, THE FAMILY, AND INDIVIDUAL."

It is almost incredible that the Prime Minister of England, with the facts of the Meath elections, can forget his reiterated opinions of 1874. In the *Vatican Decrees* he declared that he had justified his statement that "the extreme claims of the Middle Ages have been sanctioned, and have been revived without the warrant or excuse which might in those ages have been shown for them," and that "the claims asserted by the Pope are such as to place civil allegiance at his mercy." Whether this is true of the Pope now or not, it is most assuredly true of the Irish Hierarchy. And yet Mr. Gladstone is prepared to hand over all the rights, civil and religious, of the Irish people to what he believes to be the "resistless domineering action of a purely central power." This is not a common apostasy from an avowed political opinion. It is the contradiction in terms of a moral belief once held by an English Prime Minister, but now cast off like a worn-out cloak. Does Mr. Gladstone affirm and deny now the positive conclusion to which he came in 1874, when speaking of the ecclesiastical system of the Roman Catholic Church? "Of that system as a system," he said: "I must say that its influence is adverse to freedom in the State, the family, and the individual; that when weak it is too often crafty, and when strong tyrannical; and that though in this country no one could fairly deny to its professors the credit of doing what they think is for the glory of God, they exhibit in a notable degree the vast self-deluding forces which make sport of our common nature. The great instrument to which they look for the promotion of Christianity seems to be an unmeasured exaltation of the clerical class, and of its power, as against all that is secular and lay—an exaltation not less unhealthy for that order itself than for society at large."

It is against this system, and against this exaltation of the clerical power, which the Irish Protestants and the more liberal-minded Roman Catholics of Ireland are protesting to-day. They do so in the interests of freedom. "Among the many noble thoughts of Homer," said Mr. Gladstone in the concluding sentence of *Vaticanism*, "there is not one more noble or more penetrating than his judgment upon slavery. 'On the day,' he says,

> ' that makes a bondsman of the free,
> Wide-seeing Zeus takes half the man away.' "

What Homer said against servitude in the social order the Irish Loyalist and Mr. Gladstone plead against the present political tyranny of the Irish priesthood.

CHAPTER XIII.

LESSONS OF HISTORY.

WHEN the Hon. George Leveson-Gower was in search of a seat in the House of Commons in 1887, and naturally anxious to make himself acquainted with the new Liberal policy of Home Rule, Mr. Gladstone, in a memorable letter, wrote, "Dear George—study Irish History." Reading history for the purpose of finding evidence to buttress up a preconceived theory is one thing; reading history for the purpose of gaining light upon the character and probable conduct of a race under given conditions is another.

The Irish who object to Home Rule are at all events not open to the insinuation that their convictions are new and their professions prompted by mere self-interest. They and their fathers have been loyal to the Act of Union, and the landowners refused Mr. Gladstone's great bribe in 1886, which offered twenty years' purchase of their lands in exchange for their birthright of citizenship under an Imperial Parliament. They refused the bribe, and they intend to keep their birthright.

But they all also refer to history for a sound basis for their position. On two occasions only have Irishmen possessed a Parliament such as Mr. Gladstone proposed in 1886 to set up: viz., during the era of the Irish Rebellion of 1841, and during that of the Revolution of 1688-91. In each it can be shown that they exhibited the same incapacity of self-control, the same want of moderation, the same predilection for extreme measures and indefensible actions. Violence and the want of the spirit of compromise (which is so distinguishing a difference between the English and the Irish) invariably wrecked the only true Parliaments which Ireland ever had in which Roman Catholics were the dominant element.

Until the reign of King James I. the native Irish had but little part in Parliament. Parliament in Ireland was originally nothing but a Court Baron of the King's chief tenants, always depending on tenure; and the Irish in early times had no English tenures. Even after the time of James I., when the Irish had all of necessity accepted English tenure, they were overbalanced by the many new boroughs recently founded by Protestant planters. It may be said with truth that the only two real Irish Parliaments ever held were the Parliaments of the Confederation of Kilkenny (A.D. 1642-52), and that of King James II., held at the King's Inn in 1690.

In 1641 the great Irish Rebellion took place, into the causes of which it is unnecessary here to enter.

Suffice it to say that the result was that the Parliament of England at once offered the land of the Irish as security for any money that should be "adventured" for putting down the rebels. King Charles I. protested that such a law would render the Irish desperate,—that one should not "sell the bear's skin before the bear be dead,"—but nevertheless the bill was passed, for the popular party in Parliament cared little about making the Irish desperate.

The First Independent Irish Parliament.

In these circumstances the Irish, consisting then, as now, of two very discordant races, the old native Irish and the old English of Ireland (viz., the Butlers, Talbots, Cusacks, Plunkets, Prestons, and others), formed for themselves a Government of their own at Kilkenny, which was called the Confederation of Irish Catholics, consisting of a Supreme Council and a General Assembly. If ever there was need of prudent conduct, it was in this crisis of Ireland's fate, when the lands, liberties, and even lives of the Catholic Irish were at stake. And for three years, under the prudent guidance of the Anglo-Irish, things were decently managed. The Supreme Council consisted mostly of Anglo-Irish, with power to conclude treaties with foreign nations and to make peace with the King's subjects, subject always to an oath taken by each councillor and by every member of the Assembly to make no peace without "to the uttermost of his power" striving for the public exercise of the Roman Catholic religion. At this period the public hatred of England and Scotland to that religion was intense, and it was as much as the King could do, during the numerous negotiations for peace, to promise secretly through his agent, the Earl of Glamorgan, that he would grant the Catholic Irish their rights when, by the aid of their forces, he should be restored to his own.

The Pope's Nuncio.

The Duke of Ormonde, a Protestant, who was the King's Lieutenant, was the central figure of the drama. He it was who, more than any man of that day, had the confidence and good-will of both countries, and while he held the reins of power all went well. But in 1643 the Confederation determined to apply to the Pope for a Nuncio. Urban VIII. sent Rinuccini, Archbishop of Fermo, to Ireland; and with the arrival of the Nuncio began the series of events which culminated in the arrival of Cromwell. Ormonde had already concluded the best peace he could make, considering the extraordinary circumstances of England, just before the landing in Ireland of Rinuccini, in October 1645. The Nuncio, whose instructions from the Pope were to revive the Roman Catholic religion in all the freedom and splendour of Brussels and Paris, immediately set himself against Ormonde. The peace was proclaimed in August 1646. Rinuccini summoned a congregation of the clergy to Waterford, and condemned the peace, declared the parties that contracted it perjured, and excommunicated all who should support it. Such high-handed doings immediately made evident to the clear-eyed what had always existed under the outwardly united body of the Catholic Confederation. The old native Irish followed the Nuncio, who preferred to see the Parliament and the Puritans triumph rather than the King; for the King's triumph meant the triumph of Ormonde, who was a "heretic," and no heretic Viceroy would help to restore the Catholic religion in Ireland. The Anglo-Irish were naturally loyal to the Crown. They had, moreover, received grants of land from the kings of England, and they feared lest the old Irish, under the Nuncio's leadership, would assert their claim to the whole soil of Ireland. It was through fear of this claim that many Catholics of great estate avoided joining the Confederation until they were forced by circumstances into the ranks. The action of the Nuncio precipitated the divisions which had hitherto been covered over. The old Irish were set in a flame by the Pope's representative, and believed that the Nuncio was sent to free the country from the rule of heretics and to head them in a war for this purpose. They always believed that if the worst came to the worst France and Spain would come to the assistance of Ireland, to prevent the establishment of a heretical republic. The result was that all cohesion amongst Irish parties disappeared.

The Ormondists and the Nuncio's faction were at open war with each other; and Ormonde, in 1647, gave up Dublin to the Parliament of England and retired from the Viceroyalty. Again the Supreme Council of the Confederation negotiated for his return, and he came back in 1648. Again the Nuncio and the Catholic clergy excommunicated all who should serve in his ranks; Owen Roe O'Neil supporting the old Irish, and Preston supporting the Supreme Council and the Anglo-Irish. In 1649 the Nuncio fled from Ireland. But in 1650 the bishops and clergy drove away Ormonde a second time, and formed a new confederation on the principle of freedom of religion, and believed that either God or foreign nations would come to their aid. But instead there appeared upon the horizon the terrible visage and sword of Oliver Cromwell, overthrowing all Irish factions, and making the strong arm of England felt in every corner of the island.

The Modern Parallel.

The Nationalists of to-day fill exactly the part of the old Irish in the Catholic Confederation. The Irish bishops of that day rushed in, headed by the "bedlamite" Nuncio, to prevent the ratification of Ormonde's place. Religion in all its splendour, the restoration of Church and Abbey lands, their seats in the House of Lords: all that they cared for, was in question. And they accordingly excommunicated all who supported the peace. This was to boycott the loyal

Anglo-Irish Catholics of Ireland. Their successors in the Irish hierarchy have thrown themselves in the same way between owners and occupiers of land, supporting the Plan of Campaign and preventing any negotiations for peace or agreement in a social war of humble dimensions. We see Archbishops Walsh and Croke blessing the opponents of English law, and writing manifestoes urging resistance to established authority. Rinuccini insisted on the recognition of ecclesiastical immunity, and forced the Assembly of the Catholic Confederation to declare through their President that the House did not claim any power over a bishop. "It was alleged," he wrote, "that the law would allow of the imprisonment of a bishop. But the bishops protested against it." The same immunity was claimed over and over again, as has been shown by the Roman Catholic clergy of the present day during the last few years.

In this first historical illustration of the calamities engendered and wrought out by the domination of a clerical party in the State, the Ulster Protestants have an interesting as well as a very strong case.

King James II. in Ireland.

We now come to the history of the Roman Catholic Parliament in Ireland two hundred years ago. James II. ascended the throne in 1685, and on coming to the crown Ireland was in the most flourishing condition. Lands were improved, money was plentiful, trade flourished, and the revenue increased proportionately. In four short years all was desolation and misery. Driven from England, King James, assisted by France, allied himself with Tyrconnell and the Irish priesthood to play the old game of revolution, much as Mr. Gladstone is to-day allied for the same end with Archbishops Walsh and Croke and the Irish-American enemy. Everything had been carefully prepared for the king's arrival. Tyrconnell, with neither conscience, veracity nor prudence, was an unscrupulous tool, and did his work as thoroughly as was possible. As a preliminary step all the Protestant Militia were disarmed. Then all Protestants were deprived of their arms, but the Nationalists or native Irish were permitted to retain their weapons. The Army was next remodelled, and all Protestants were excluded from service. The majority went abroad and took service under William. Then came radical changes in the Courts of Law. One Alexander Fitton, who had been detected in forgery in England, was brought over by Tyrconnell and made Lord Chancellor. The Protestant judges were nearly all superseded by Roman Catholics, and throughout Ireland Tyrconnell secured to his creatures the execution of the laws and the nomination of juries. Mr. Healy and his party are aiming at the same thing to-day. In 1687 there was but one Protestant Sheriff appointed in all Ireland. The corporations were the next victims. New charters were granted; and in each, slaves to Tyrconnell were stuffed in, in room of the Protestants. When the Privy Council was entirely remodelled in the same direction the cup of the Loyalists was full. The whole military, civil, and administrative power in the country was at last transferred to the native Nationalist Irish. After four years they had brought the land to desolation. The destruction of property was almost incredible; cattle were slaughtered in mere wantonness, and the Protestants computed their losses at eight millions of money. The rapparees were the lords of Ireland, and flattered themselves that very soon not a Protestant would be left in the country. Such was the state of affairs when James landed in Kinsale on March 12th, 1689.

He reached Dublin on the 24th, where he was received by the Roman Catholic hierarchy and passed into the Castle, from which a banner waved with the inscription "Now or never: now and for ever"—a motto revived by J. Fintan Lalor in his celebrated sketch plan of agrarian insurrection in 1848.

The object of the Irish party two centuries ago was the threefold one which is sure to make its appearance in every Irish agitation whatever may have been its commencement: viz., Roman Catholic ascendency, separation from Great Britain, and the possession of the land. At this crisis in 1689 the Irish Nationalist party had already attained Roman Catholic ascendency, and were making their preparations for a Parliament which should fully carry out Irish ideas. The first

Irish idea then, as now, was that Roman Catholic Ireland should never be governed by Protestant England. The hour was now come: in 1689 a Parliament assembled in Dublin, which has ever since remained a curiosity of history.

The House, of course, was packed with Tyrconnell and his creatures; 232 members were returned. Six only were Protestants. To his credit be it stated that James was not in favour of repealing the Acts of Settlement, but his expostulations and remonstrances only irritated the Irish. They even accused him of being a Protestant. They determined to have the land back again; and accordingly a bill for repealing the Acts of Settlement was passed with a hurrah only to be paralleled in an assembly of nineteenth-century Nationalists on the point of confiscating the property of the present landowners. Twelve millions of acres were transferred to King James' Nationalists, and the beggaring and ruin of the Irish Protestants was complete. The Irish legislature next forced the King to agree to the Act of Attainder. By this act 2445 persons practically—the whole Protestant nobility, gentry and traders of Ireland—were attainted of high treason, proscribed by name, and their personal property was confiscated. Next were confiscated all the endowments of the Protestant Church, and the church fabrics throughout the country were also seized. Protestantism was to be destroyed, and accordingly innumerable oppressions were committed to that end with the approval of the Executive. Anarchy reigned supreme, while James and his allies attempted to "make Ireland a nation" under the protection of a foreign power. Had not William the Deliverer conquered this Nationalist rising, and rescued Ireland from the hands of the "patriots," the British colony would have been wiped out.

How is forgetfulness of such a chapter of history possible for the descendants of the men who suffered under this tyranny and helped powerfully to overturn it? What is bred in the bone is bound to come out in the flesh; and not all the oratory of Mr. Gladstone, not all the guarantees of a paper Constitution, not all the assurances of the Archangel Gabriel himself, will convince the Irish Protestants to-day that it is good for them to be thrust out from the citizenship of a United Kingdom and placed under the rule of a Roman Catholic Parliament in Dublin. History has repeated itself too often in Ireland not to make it possible that it may be repeated again.

CHAPTER XIV.

THE CANADIAN PRIEST IN POLITICS.

THOSE who desire to see an object lesson in Home Rule cannot do better than turn their eyes to the province of Quebec in the Dominion of Canada. The population is mainly Roman Catholic, descended from the old French colonists; and although the constitution is as democratic as it can be, there is only one great power existing, and that is the power of the priest. Ireland, under Cardinal Logue and Archbishop Walsh, is accurately foreshadowed in Quebec. Ultramontanism is supreme, and the Jesuits are the real governors of the province. Let those who desire to understand to what extent this is true consult Mr. Goldwin Smith's book, *Canada and the Canadian Question.* "Quebec is a theocracy," he writes. "While Rome has been losing her hold on Old France and on all the European nations, she has retained, nay, tightened, it here. The people are the sheep of the priest. He is their political as well as their spiritual chief, and nominates the politician who serves the interest of the Church at Quebec or at Ottawa. The faith of the peasantry is mediæval."

The Power of the Church in Canada.

The population of Quebec is about 1,500,000, of which a very small minority is Protestant, whose numbers the stern logic of events has tended to diminish. The French Canadians breed quickly. As in Ireland, the priests encourage early marriages and discourage emigration. The Legislature even has gone so far as to offer, as a reward, the grant of one hundred acres of land to any family boasting twelve or more children. The claimants numbered over a thousand! Here would be an interesting precedent for a Home Rule Government, who would be naturally anxious to increase the patriotic population of their native land. "While the people are poor, the Church is," says Mr. Goldwin Smith, "for such a country, immensely rich. Not Versailles or the Pyramids bespoke the power of the king more clearly than the great Church and the monastery rising above the cabins bespeak the power of the priest. A hundred millions of dollars (£22,000,000) would probably be a low estimate of her realised property, while her annual income is reckoned at ten millions. Masses for souls are everywhere a source of revenue to her. She is always investing with profit. Besetting the people from the cradle to the grave, with her friars and nuns she daily gathers in money, of which none ever leaves her coffers, even for taxes, *since she asserts her sacred immunity from taxation.* Lotteries, in spite of their affinity to gambling, are sanctioned to add to the Holy Fund."

THE INCIDENCE OF TAXATION.

With such conditions it is natural that the Roman Catholic Church in Quebec should use its power in the Legislature to lay the principal burden of taxation where it will not touch its own pocket. Mr. T. W. Russell, M.P., has given a graphic sketch of the way this has been managed. Writing in the *Scotsman*, he says :—

"The fact is, the exactions of a rapacious and rich Church have ruined the peasantry. They are steeped in poverty. They can and do contribute little or nothing to the provincial revenues. The treasury of the province is empty. Her debt rolls up. And the only resource left is a raid upon the Englishry of Montreal. Thus we have all kinds of ecclesiastical property exempt from taxation—municipal and provincial—whilst every commercial company is taxed, the minimum tax on a limited company being $600. Nor is the system of taxation fair. The Bank of Montreal, for example, is taxed for Quebec purposes on its full capital. And it is, of course, taxed elsewhere in some other way. As for the municipality, the case is said to be even more glaring. Nine-tenths of the commerce of the province is in the hands of the Englishry. It would be much more correct to say that it is in the hands of the Scotch, for Scotsmen are at the head of everything. The railways, the banks, the insurance companies, the shipping, the land trusts, the large warehouses—everything of the kind is English or Scottish. In Montreal the English, French, and Irish quarters are separate and apart. The Englishry are taxed to the throat—the others practically go scot free. And whenever a deficiency occurs a raid is made on the commercial classes. Of course, there is always a fresh valuation. But, all the same, the raid is made, and it is safe to say that this comparatively small portion of the population bears five-sixths of the city and provincial taxation. If ever there was an object lesson for Ulster, it is to be found in Quebec. Here we have the Celtic race; here we have the Roman Catholic Church, at once a Christian institution and a political machine; here we have Home Rule in all its fulness *plus* paid members of Parliament and plenty of them. And certainly the Canadians in Quebec are not happy."

THE CLAIM OF ECCLESIASTICAL IMMUNITY.*

Instances have already been given in a former chapter of the claims which Roman Catholic priests in Ireland have made during the past years to stand above the law. In Quebec, however, these claims have been carried still further.

In the year 1876 an election petition against the

* Article on "Canada and Canadian Institutions," *Scotsman*, Jan. 12th, 1893.

return of Sir Hector Langevin took place in the province of Quebec. The case came on for hearing before one of Her Majesty's judges—Judge Routhier, a Roman Catholic. Among the witnesses summoned on subpœna was the Rev. M. Cinq-Mars curé of St. Simon's. This ecclesiastic addressed the court as follows :—

"In accordance with the instructions forwarded to all parish priests at the same time as the last pastoral letter of the bishops of the Province of Quebec, it would be my duty respectfully to deny the competence of this tribunal. Nevertheless, as I am accused by a false witness named Johnny Desbians, and leave has been granted by my bishop, the Archbishop of Quebec, to all parish priests of Chalevoix to appear as witnesses in this case by a letter addressed to the counsel for the defendant, and the parish priests of the country, I, of my own free will, come forward to give my evidence ; nevertheless recording my protest."

Notwithstanding this impudent statement the trial proceeded, and in his summing up the judge proceeded to deal with the claim made by the curé of St. Simon's, and, in doing so, made the following astounding observations :—

"Immunity '*de persona*' is the privilege of the competent court. It is personal, inherent in every ecclesiastical person, and consists in its not being possible that that ecclesiastical person should be accused or cited for trial before any but an ecclesiastical court. The personal immunity of the priest extends to all cases, whatever be their nature, save a few rare exceptions which it would be too long to enumerate. Whether he may have acted as a priest or as a citizen in his public life, or as an individual in his private life, he is always an ecclesiastical person —he enjoys the privilege of a competent court, that is to say, he can decline the competency of any lay court. Such is the Catholic doctrine, and I can give its substance in a few words. I am incompetent in all cases where the question to be decided is one of dogmatic doctrine, of morals or discipline, and also in those cases where the person prosecuted is an ecclesiastic. I am competent to judge the actions of a priest so far as they affect the interests of third parties, provided that the actions are of a temporal description and that the person of the priest is not involved."

The Claim Dismissed on Appeal.

Finally the judge dismissed the petition. The petitioners promptly appealed to the Supreme Court of Canada, and the moment the case came before the Court the judgment was of course reversed and the appeal allowed.

It may be thought by some that Judge Routhier's dictum was only the eccentricity of one ill-informed bigoted man. It seems hard to believe that any of Her Majesty's judges in any part of the British Empire should deliberately go back to a condition of things which was generally supposed to be put an end to by the Constitutions of Clarendon, some six hundred years ago, for his views of the rights of Her Majesty's courts.

But unfortunately we are left in no doubt at all upon this matter. The judgment delivered by Judge Routhier was a correct expression of the doctrine of the Roman Catholic Church—a doctrine which has always found, and will always find, its expression in every country where the authorities of the Roman Catholic Church are sufficiently free from civilised public opinion to dare to enforce it.

The Bishops Condemn the Judgment.

The decision of the Supreme Court was followed by a "Declaration" by the bishops of the province of Quebec, in which, after mentioning the rights of the Church as an instructor in all matters, they refer to and condemn the judgment of the Supreme Court. They particularly selected for condemnation the following paragraph in that judgment:—

"I admit without the slightest hesitation, and with the fullest conviction, the right of the Catholic priest to preach and define religious dogma and every point of ecclesiastical discipline. I deny to him in the present case, as well as in every similar one, the right to point out an individual as a political party, and to hold the one or the other to public indignation by accusing it of Catholic liberalism or any other religious error. Above all, I deny him the right to say that any one who may assist in the election of such a candidate will commit a heinous sin."

It should be noted that the Roman Catholic judges of the Supreme Court entirely concurred with the judgment of their Protestant brothers. This action on their part raised a storm of indignation among the priests' party. The excommunication of the offending judges was demanded, nor was the trouble put an end to until a special delegate had been sent over by the Pope to inquire into the whole question—an inquiry which led to an order from the Vatican enjoining clerical abstention from all interference in elections.

A Canadian Priest on Lay Obedience.

As to the view which the priests themselves in Lower Canada take of their spiritual duties, it does not appear that it materially differs from that adopted by several of the priests in Meath. Here, for instance, is the view expressed by the curé of L'Ile Bizard in the instructions issued by him to his flock :—

"I am here on purpose to guide you; and if you do not do as I tell you, you will be damned. For, mind you, I was appointed your curé by the bishop, who in his turn was appointed by the Pope, and he (the Pope), you know very well, was appointed by God. Therefore, when you do not do as I tell you, when you do not listen to me, you do not listen to God; and if you do not listen to the voice of God through me, you will be damned. Remember, we have had two sudden deaths in this parish during the week. Were these people prepared? I do not know. But remember you may also die suddenly. Are you going to prepare yourselves to meet your God, your Sovereign Judge, by voting for the enemies of His Church?"

Such are some of the features of the conduct of Canadian priests in politics, and they prove conclusively that the same spirit of intolerance and mediæval despotism exists on both sides of the Atlantic.

What has happened under Home Rule in Quebec is most likely to happen in Ireland. The analogy is striking if not absolutely complete. There is the demand of the priesthood for legislative independence, which, since 1867 in Quebec, has secured to the Roman Catholic Church in that province unlimited power. That power has been used to boycott public opinion, to tax the great industries which are in the hands of the Protestant minority, and to enable the Church to become enormously wealthy. Quite lately the Roman Catholic majority in Quebec passed an Act endowing the Jesuits out of public property. What has been done with regard to Montreal, the seat of those industries, may well be expected to be done with regard to Belfast. And political corruption has followed in the train of this combination of Home Rule and Ultramontanism.

"Mr. Mercier has risen," said Mr. Goldwin Smith in 1891, "to lead Ultramontanism and Nationalism at once, and has been raised by their joint forces to the premiership of the province. He proclaims himself the devout liegeman of the Pope, wears a papal decoration on his breast, seeks the papal blessing before going into an election contest, champions all ecclesiastical claims, restores the Jesuits to their estates, and boasts to a great Roman Catholic assemblage at Baltimore that he has thereby redressed the wrong done by George III." Since then Mr. Mercier has been driven from power, leaving behind him an almost bankrupt treasury, and the necessity of fresh taxation, while charges of wholesale jobbery and corruption taint the whole political atmosphere. Such is Home Rule in Quebec; and in Quebec, as in Ireland, the hand that grasps political power is that of the Roman Catholic priest.

CHAPTER XV.

THE ATTITUDE OF IRISH PROTESTANTISM.

WHEN the bill for the Disestablishment of the Church of Ireland in 1869 was passing through its third reading Mr. Disraeli spoke of the effect of that measure upon the aims and objects of the Papacy. He prophesied that it would take advantage of the new departure to advance its opinions and its political authority. Then he went on to say :—

"Will the Protestants of Ireland submit to the establishment of Papal ascendency without a struggle ? It may occur probably when the Union of the two countries, which is to be partially dissolved to-night, may be completely destroyed; for it is very possible that after a period of great disquietude, doubt and passion, events may occur which may complete that severance of the Union which to-night we are commencing. What I fear is that it may lead to civil war. It is natural and probable that the Papal power in Ireland will attempt to attain ascendency and predominance. I say it is natural, and what is more, it ought to do it, and it will do it. Is it natural that the

Protestants of Ireland should submit without a struggle to such a state of things? You know they will not. Is England to interfere? Are we to have a repetition of the direful history which on both sides now we desire to forget? Is there to be another battle of the Boyne, another siege of Derry, another Treaty of Limerick? These things are not only possible, but probable."

If such catastrophes appeared possible and probable in 1869 to the far-seeing eye of an English statesman, can any one say that they are not actually impending with the slow but awful certitude of a moving avalanche? Mr. John Morley endeavoured, on the eve of the Belfast Convention in 1892, to laugh away the fears of Irish Protestants. "What," said he, "are these men afraid of? I never can get an answer to that question." In these pages some attempt has been made to answer Mr. Morley. His effort to reduce the case of the Irish Protestants to an absurdity failed most signally, and is perhaps an adequate measure of a philosopher's statesmanship.

"There was an exhibition," he said, "the other day in Maddox Street of instruments of mediæval torture. Do they expect the Irish Parliament is going to revive the cruelties of the Inquisition, and rekindle the fires of Smithfield? It is nonsense. Everybody knows it is nonsense."

Is boycotting nonsense? Are the penalties of non-compliance with the edict of boycotting nonsense? Is not boycotting under clerical sanction rather the revival of the Inquisition scientifically wrought out and worked as cruelly and relentlessly as ever the system was in Spain? Mr. Morley talks of the fires of Smithfield and the impossibility of their revival. It may be so. But the revelations of the Meath petition demonstrate that at the end of the nineteenth century the spirit of persecution lives and burns as fiercely in Ireland as ever it did in England in the days of Bloody Mary. Such attempts to palter with the situation are unworthy of any man claiming to be a statesman.

THE CHURCH OF IRELAND.

Rightly or wrongly, the Irish Protestants are practically unanimous at this great crisis of Ireland's history upon the subject of Home Rule. Let us review the action of the various Protestant communities taken and repeated ofttimes during the past seven years. In 1886 the Protestant Episcopal Church of Ireland held a special General Synod, composed of two archbishops and ten bishops, 208 clerical and 416 lay members. This body represented 600,000 people in every district and parish in Ireland. The widespread distribution of these Protestants can be imagined when it is said that a quarter of a million live in the three provinces outside Ulster. This Synod passed unanimously resolutions against Home Rule, and declared that such a measure would aggravate the peril to civil and religious liberty, and the insecurity of life and property, which even then existed. The debate upon these resolutions was most striking, and is well worthy of reference and reconsideration.

"It is the thing, not the name, we object to," said the Bishop of Derry. "Our gorge rises at the tartar emetic, though the doctor soothingly calls it antimonial wine. We desire to remain an integral part of an Imperial people. We and our fathers have lived under the shadow of a great tree, the stately growth of a thousand summers. We will not exchange it for a place under a tree which sophists and experimentalists have taken a fancy to plant head downwards, whose sure fall will crush us amidst the inextinguishable laughter of the world."

THE NONCONFORMIST CHURCHES OF IRELAND.

In March 1886 official addresses were presented by all the Protestant Churches in Ireland to Lord Aberdeen expressing the same sentiment. The Presbyterian Church, numbering 500,000; the Non-Subscribing Presbyterians, 60,000; and the Methodist Church, numbering 51,000, all declared their belief that under a separate Parliament civil and religious liberty would be endangered, and the present system of education in Ireland would be altered to the detriment of the Protestant bodies.

In 1888 an address was presented to Lord Salisbury and Lord Hartington by the ministers of the Nonconformist Churches in Ireland on November 14th, deprecating in the strongest manner, as disastrous to the best interests of the country, a separate Parliament for Ireland. "We do not believe," said the address, "that any guarantees, moral or material, could be devised which would safeguard the right of minorities scattered throughout Ireland." Out of a total of 990 Nonconformist ministers of all denominations, 864 signed the address. Only eight declared themselves Home Rulers, and the remainder mostly declined on the ground that being ministers of religion they wished to have nothing to do with politics.

The significance of their address, as the Moderator, Mr. Lynd, said, was emphasised by the fact that until Mr. Gladstone abandoned the Liberalism of the greater part of his political life, at least 95 per cent. of the ministers of his Church were his most ardent and devoted adherents. Indeed, out of the 600 Presbyterian ministers, he questioned whether they could have found more than a dozen who were not supporters of Mr. Gladstone's policy. The same might have been said of the other Irish Nonconformist bodies. They had not surrendered their Liberalism, but Mr. Gladstone had marched with colours flying into the Parnellite camp, and put himself at the head of the Parnellite forces, and they declined to follow him.

A Methodist on the Crisis.

The Rev. Henry Evans, D.D., on behalf of the Methodist Church, said :—

"As regards my own Church, my Lords, its right is that of a body across whose shield the bar sinister has never been drawn—a body on whose escutcheon there is not a blot—a body whose Christian service and honourable citizenship history dares not challenge. Our right to be heard on behalf of our country is that of a Church among whose members there is the smallest percentage of illiteracy—is that of a Church of whose members, I believe, there is not one in jail in all Ireland—is that of a Church whose people are not in the 'workhouse' or a burden to the rates. We neither manufacture criminals nor paupers, nor have we ever obliged the state to expend a sixpence to make us loyal. Our 'local knowledge' tells us that Mr. Gladstone cannot say the same of his Fenian protegés and Parnellite allies, out of whose 'circles' and 'branches' his proposed government of Ireland would be framed. Nor is our support of the Union due to any financial interest which we draw from it. We have no endowments, and never had. There is nothing in the way of office to purchase our allegiance. Christianity and patriotism alone inspire and dictate our loyalty to the Union, for under Imperial administration alone can the equilibrium and tranquil equipoise of rival interests be secured to Ireland. My Lords, I have been asked to indicate the hurt which a Parnellite Government would do to Ireland. It would inevitably put education under the priesthood; and I ask English Nonconformists how they would like that for themselves in England?"

These sentiments were again endorsed at the Irish Methodist Conference in June 1892.

In 1890 the Irish Presbyterian Church made a further declaration against Home Rule, contained in an address to the Presbyterian and the Nonconformist bodies in Great Britain; signed by the Moderator, the Rev. W. Park. Individually and in their corporate capacity the Irish Protestants have continued in season and out of season to urge their views upon the people of Great Britain.

Appeal to British Nonconformists.

The following is an extract from the appeal sent to British Nonconformists at the General Election of 1892 by their Irish brethren, and it sets forth with great plainness the feelings of Irish Protestants upon Mr. Gladstone's proposals :—

"Being at a distance, you possibly do not appreciate the power which the Roman Catholic bishops and priests have over the great bulk of Irish Roman Catholics, and the determination which they display to compel obedience to their directions in temporal as well as in spiritual matters. The Roman Catholic hierarchy claim the right to direct their people in all proceedings where the interests of Catholicity are involved, and also to determine for their people what are the proceedings which affect the interests of their Church. This is, in effect, a claim on the part of the hierarchy to govern Ireland, in which the Roman

Catholic population is in a majority; and under a system of Home Rule they would be enabled to do so. We believe that no guarantees, moral or material, can be devised which will guard the rights of the Protestant minorities which are scattered throughout Ireland against the encroachments of a Roman Catholic majority endowed with legislative and executive powers, and thus directed by their clergy. History, as well as experience, in this and other lands, assure us of this. We accordingly feel that the proposal to give Ireland Home Rule most seriously threatens our religious liberties, which would in numberless ways be imperilled under an Irish National Parliament, the majority in which would be elected on the nomination of the Roman Catholic priests. Judging from the past, such a Parliament would claim and exercise the right to tax Protestants for the maintenance of educational institutions in the direct interests of Roman Catholicism, would legalise the desecration of the Lord's day, and would ultimately establish and endow the Roman Catholic religion in Ireland. From these and many other evils we are preserved by the Imperial Parliament."

Views of the Rev. J. Parker.

This appeal met with the approval and sympathy of no less a person than the Rev. Joseph Parker, a well-known London Congregationalist and a follower of Mr. Gladstone. He said:—

"We rightly listen to appeals from Eastern Christians and from oppressed nationalities: why, then, pay no heed to the statements of our fellow-subjects? If they are few in number, the more need they may have of our help. If their Protestantism is the cause of their alarm, this only confirms their place in our own historical succession. We cannot separate ourselves from our Ulster brethren. Nonconformity is one and the same all the world over. It is not for the hand to ignore the foot, or the eye to ignore the ear : we hold a common principle, and we must unite in a common demand. No greater disaster could befall us than the creation of one kind of Nonconformity in England and another in Ireland." *

Only a few selections have been made from the great mass of utterances which have been given forth from Protestant Ireland. The voice of Protestant Ireland, however, was heard unequivocally at the Belfast Convention; and that historic event deserves, and must receive, separate treatment. Meanwhile the views of Ulstermen have been admirably put in the *Spectator* by an "Irish Nonconformist." He said :—

"Since the Union, and during this present century, what has been called 'Greater Britain' has been formed, and India has become an Empire. Owing to the fact that Irishmen have had fewer openings in their own country than either Englishmen or Scotchmen have had in theirs, the descendants of these men have

* *Times*, June 20th, 1892.

sought employment in all parts of the world under the British flag. In India they have risen to the very highest positions, and have done, I really believe, more in proportion to their numbers to build up our great Empire than either Englishmen or Scotchmen. The result is that now we, the Unionists of Ireland, are intensely proud of the Empire and its flag, which we have helped to carry to victory in all parts of the world. We are proud of the Colonies which we have helped to form and to civilise and to govern. We are proud that Lord Wolseley, Lord Roberts, and now Sir George White, all Irish Unionists, are among the principal guardians of Britain's power. We are proud of the life-work of Lords Dufferin, Mayo, and Lawrence, and a host of other Irishmen who have represented and strengthened the Empire in various lands. And we, who are the descendants of the men who were represented in the Irish Parliaments of the last century, are now proud to be equal citizens with Englishmen and Scotchmen in the United Parliament, and with equal rights in the management of the great Empire which we have materially helped to form. In fact, we now feel ourselves to be a part of the Mother-country from which this Empire has sprung. If you take this position from us and put us under an Irish Parliament, in which we cannot have any power except by opposing England and her interests and acting entirely for our own safety, you may be as sure as you can be of anything which has not taken place, that we shall be in Ireland England's bitterest political foes; and as sure as there is a tribute imposed upon Ireland by England over which we have no control, it will be a source of intense bitterness which will lead to future trouble of which the Gladstonian Liberals have now apparently no thought. A son turned out of his father's house when he has been doing his duty, in order to try to win another son who has been disloyal to his family, cannot have kindly feelings towards those who have so ill-treated him. This is what the Gladstonian Liberals are now trying to do with us. We love the British flag and all that it represents. It is the symbol to us of liberty, power, and unity. There is not a Nationalist Member of Parliament who dare exhibit this flag in Ireland. The Unionists, who are British in their feelings and conduct, are to be turned out in order to try to buy the favour of those who would wish to see the Empire destroyed and England humiliated."*

* *Spectator*, Feb. 4th, 1893.

CHAPTER XVI.

THE SCOT IN ULSTER.

ULSTER is largely a Scottish colony. The very foundation of civilised society in the North of Ireland is Scottish; "It is the solid granite on which it rests." Throughout the great reign of Elizabeth Ulster was the scene of one long horror in which the sword, the famine, and the pestilence played their grisly parts. The Irish chiefs were crushed, their lands confiscated, and Ireland for the first time was brought under the dominion of England. When James I. came to the throne the country had been completely conquered, and the ravages of war were succeeded by the quietude of death. Those were the days of "high emprise" and daring adventure. For centuries the warlike Scot had gone forth to play the part of the mercenary soldier in the armies of Europe, while his English brother had been laying the foundation of the British Empire. Deprived by the union of the two kingdoms under a Scottish King of his favourite domestic occupation of civil war, the Scot turned his attention to Ulster.

THE FIRST SCOTCH COLONIES.

The northern half of Down, now represented in

Parliament by Major Waring, was the first part of Ulster to be colonised. James Hamilton and Hugh Montgomery received grants of Irish land on the express condition that they should plant it with Scotch and English colonists, and they carried out their undertaking to the letter. These planters were Presbyterians then, and they remain Presbyterians unto this day. The success of this colony was immediate. Eight years after the Scots had made good their footing in this northeast corner of Ireland, a contemporary letter showed that Hamilton and Montgomery had above two thousand men able to bear arms in King James's service, a number which represented an emigration of at least ten thousand souls. The men were ploughing virgin soil and planting trees, building homesteads and ditching lands that had before never known a boundary. The women were spinning and the girls knitting. The sun had arisen at last on an industrial corner of Ireland, where a new race of men was to live and thrive under the ægis of the British Parliament and of no other.

The next colony was planted across the River Logan in South Antrim, now represented by Mr. W. Ellison Macartney. In 1603, Sir Arthur Chichester, Lord Deputy of Ireland, obtained a grant of the Castle of Bealfaste, or Belfast, together with the lands of lower Clanneboye. These he let largely to officers of his army; and what is now covered by the southern portion of Belfast was first leased to Moses Hill, the ancestor of the present Marquis of Downshire. South

Antrim was mainly planted by English settlers, and North Antrim was peaceably settled owing to the action of the Irish Chieftain Randal Macdonnel, who after Tyrone's rebellion threw his lot in with the Government and turned loyal subject. When King James created him Earl of Antrim, the patent specially mentioned the fact that he had strenuously exerted himself "in settling British subjects on his estates."

Unchanged and Unchangeable.

The plantations in Down and Antrim were thorough in their beginning and in their results. They are as much Scotch and English counties to-day as Dumfries or Cumberland. Take the polls at the general election in 1892 and they prove it. In North Antrim Mr. C. Connor, thrice Lord Mayor of Belfast, was returned by a majority of 2,639. Mid-Antrim returned Hon. Robert T. O'Neill unopposed, while his majority in 1886 was 3,698. South Antrim did the same for Captain McCalmont both in 1886 and 1892; and Mr. Macartney has also been invariably elected unopposed in South Antrim since 1885. County Down is also strongly British, almost unanimous in its opinions. Out of four divisions, three members were returned unopposed in 1892 to fight against Repeal of the Union—viz., Colonel Waring for North Down, Right Honourable Lord A. Hill for West Down, and Mr. J. A. Rentoul, Q.C., for East Down. In South Down Mr. M. M'Cartan was elected as a Nationalist by a majority of 571. In these two counties, therefore, there is an overwhelming majority of votes thrown to protest against the attempt to tear the descendants of English and Scotch colonists out of the niche they have for three centuries occupied in the heart of the British Constitution.

THE GREAT PLANTATION OF ULSTER.

The plantations of Down and Antrim, however, were insignificant as compared with the great plantation of Ulster for which King James's reign is particularly famous. The Irish chieftains, Tyrone and Tyrconnell, rightly or wrongly, were accused of plots against the Government. There was no rebellion; but the earls, either conscious of guilt, or, quite as likely, distrusting tribunals which were systematically and notoriously partial, took flight, and no less than six counties were confiscated: Londonderry, Donegal, Tyrone, Cavan, Armagh and Fermanagh were thus planted with Scotch and English colonists. In this manner was Ulster "shired" by the strong hand of King James I. Nor did he omit to show mercy on the day of victory. In the eyes of the English the measures taken were essential if the North of Ireland, till then the great obstacle to complete subjugation of the country, was to be brought fully under the dominion of English law, and if its resources were to be developed. And the assignment of a large part of the land to native owners distinguished it broadly (says

Mr. Lecky) and favourably from similar acts in previous times. It would be idle to deny that the plantation of Ulster was looked upon by the native Irish as a confiscation of their land, a breaking up of their oldest customs and traditions, and a planting amongst them of a new and a conquering race professing a hostile creed. But, as Mr. Lecky remarks, "to trace the causes whether for good or for evil that have made nations what they are is the true philosophy of history." The conquest of Ireland was carried out by a policy and by methods which cannot be defended by the standard of the nineteenth century. But the ultimate result of that conquest is what alone we have to deal with to-day.

A Distinct Nation.

Great Britain's colonies in the north of Ireland form now a nation absolutely distinct from the race which inhabits the south and west. "Compare," —says Mr. John Harrison, the author of *The Scot in Ulster*,—" Compare the political map of the Ulster of to-day with that of three centuries ago. It makes the reader feel how brief a period three centuries is in the history of races. For the north of Ireland is now very much what the first half of the seventeenth century made it. North Down and Antrim, with the great city of Belfast, are English and Scottish now as they then became, and desire to remain united with the countries from whom they sprang. South Down, on the other hand, was not planted, and it is Roman Catholic and Nationalist. Londonderry County too is loyalist, for emigrants poured into it through Coleraine and Londonderry City. Northern Armagh was peopled with English and Scottish emigrants, who crowded into it from Antrim and Down, and it desires union with the other island. Tyrone County is all strongly Unionist. But it is the country round Strabane, which the Hamiltons of Abercorn and the Stewarts of Garlies so thoroughly colonised, and the eastern portion on the borders of Lough Neagh, round the colonies formed by Lord Ochiltree, that give to the Unionists a majority. In Eastern Donegal, which the Cunninghams and Stewarts "settled" from Ayrshire and Galloway; and in Fermanagh, where dwell the descendants of Englishmen who fought so nobly in 1689, there is a great minority which struggles against separation from England. Over the rest even of Ulster the desire for a separate kingdom of Ireland is the dream of the people still as it was three centuries ago."

The Fortunes of the Colonists in Seventeenth and Eighteenth Centuries.

Why, it may be asked, have the Scotch and English colonies in Ulster never become absorbed into the native population, as the other settlements in other parts of Ireland undoubtedly have? The answer is, that there was the double cleavage of religion and race. The Presbyterian Church of Ireland was founded by Calvinists, and their stern creed forbade any mingling with the native Irish. The south-west of Scotland, from which the Ulster Scot largely came, was intensely Presbyterian, and in the history of these colonists it will be found that in their new home they were prepared to suffer and did suffer at the hands of England for the sake of their creed. But even if the great difference of religion had not effectually kept the two races apart, the convulsions of history must have done so automatically. It was in Ulster that the greatest fury of the Irish Rebellion of 1641 was felt, for there the confiscations of land were principally felt. However historians have differed in details, the main facts of the Great Rebellion are pretty well established. Those who wish to study the question are referred to Mr. Lecky, who says: "No impartial writer will deny that the rebellion in Ulster was extremely savage and bloody, though it is certainly not true that its barbarities were either unparalleled or unprovoked. They were for the most part the unpremeditated acts of a half-savage populace."* But the traditions of 1641 are still alive in the hearts of the Ulster Loyalists.

The religious wars which followed completed the utter separation of the two races. "A period of weltering confusion," says Mr. Goldwin Smith, "ensued. While the wavering struggle between the King and the Parliament was going on in England, four factions,

* Lecky's "History of England in the 18th Century," vol. i., p. 143.

like four vipers twining together in inextricable entanglements, fought, conspired, and intrigued in Ireland—the Catholic Confederates, the Catholic Nobility of the Pope, the Protestant Royalists and the Parliamentarians." The effect of such scenes had their necessary influence upon the Northern Protestant settlers. When there came additional experience of the Roman Catholic Parliament of James II. it is not surprising that King William was hailed as a deliverer in Ulster.

For some years after the Revolution a steady stream of Scotch Presbyterians poured into Ireland, and in 1715 Archbishop Synge estimated that fifty thousand Scotch families had settled in Ulster since the landing of William. The irony of history is proverbial. There were penal laws enacted against the Presbyterians of Ulster in the reign of Queen Anne, and the result was that thousands left the shores of Ireland for America, where they and their descendants subsequently took a leading part in the American revolution. It is possible even that history may repeat itself in this particular if the Ulster colony of England is treated with contempt and contumely by the parent country.

In all his recent reading of Irish history, Mr. Gladstone has never arrived at a more extraordinary half-truth than when he described the Protestants of Ulster in the Ante-Union days as ardent Nationalists. It is perfectly true that the Presbyterians of Ulster were disaffected to a very considerable extent during the eighteenth century, owing to their treatment in the matter of land and religion. The revolt of the American Colonies had a powerful reflex effect upon them, for in it were engaged thousands of Ulstermen who had been driven out of Ireland by persecution. The root and motive of rebellion in the north of Ireland was more the necessity for the abolition of terrible political grievances and religious disabilities than the dream of setting up an independent republic such as Wolfe Tone plotted to gain. The French Revolution fanned the flame, and the Society of United Irishmen was founded in Belfast and culminated in the Rebellion of 1798. But the strongly-marked cleavage of the two races had already reasserted itself. Suspicions arose in the north that the movement was to be a Roman Catholic revolution, and in 1795 the Orange Society was formed. Fierce religious animosities soon divided the Catholics and Protestants, and in the prostration and exhaustion which followed the Rebellion of 1798 the Parliament of Ireland was swept away.

Ulster Since the Union.

Whatever opinions may be held as to the necessities of the Union or the methods in which it was carried there can be no doubt that since 1800 Ulster has advanced by leaps and bounds. In trade, manufactures and science, in war and diplomacy, the descendants of the English and Scottish colonists of Ulster have made their mark on the Empire. Belfast, which was a town of some 20,000 inhabitants at the beginning of the century, is now the third port in the United Kingdom, its Customs dues being surpassed only by London and Liverpool.* Such, then, are the men who protest against their lives, liberties, and property being placed at the mercy of the Irish Nationalist party.

* "Belfast at the time of the Union had only 3000 inhabited houses, but now there were 56,000. The inhabitants had increased from 19,000 to 275,000. The shipping that came to the port at that time was 53,000 tons; it was now 2,310,000 tons. The Customs duties had increased from £101,000 to more than £2,000,000, and were only exceeded by those of Liverpool and London. The linen industry had also enormously increased. The whole of the increase in the prosperity of the town was entirely due to the working population. In his constituency there were 12,000 electors, and of these 10,000 were working men; and although they fully sympathised with the trade unions in England, they were as earnestly and sincerely opposed to Home Rule and separation as were the landlords, for they felt that their prosperity could not continue if they were cut off from Great Britain and put under the power of a hostile Assembly in Dublin. Belfast had no natural advantages, and had to import everything—coal, iron, and even a very large portion of the flax used. This increase by leaps and bounds showed that the connection with England had not affected the business of the north of Ireland, and why should not the laws which were good enough for Ulster, be good enough for the rest of Ireland? The soil was not fertile, but the agriculture there was as good as anywhere else in the country. They did not believe in the saving help of Governments, Parliaments, or Legislative Councils; all they wanted was to be let alone."—Mr. WOLFF (House of Commons), *Times*, Feb. 14th.

The valuation of Belfast in 1862 was £279,067; in 1893, £761,821, or an increase of £482,754 in thirty-one years. Up-

Their characteristics are courage, energy and a dour determination to abide by their convictions. A race of this fibre is hard to beat when fully roused.

wards of £1,000,000 has been spent in improving the harbour. The capital invested in the linen trade is £16,000,000, while the wages paid in the shipbuilding yards every week varies from £10,000 to £12,000.

CHAPTER XVII.

THE VOICE OF ULSTER AT THE BELFAST CONVENTION.

ON June 17th, 1892, United Ulster met in the city of Belfast and delivered itself in terms distinct and emphatic upon the subject of Home Rule. It pronounced a judgment upon Mr. Gladstone's policy and sent a message of appeal and warning to Great Britain. No parallel can be found in the political history of this century for the character and magnitude of the Belfast Convention of Loyal Irishmen. There were 11,879 delegates present from every parish in the province, each an elector chosen by his fellow-electors. No building was adequate to accommodate such a vast concourse of people, and consequently it was agreed that one should be built for the purpose. This structure covered 33,000 square feet, and was built of wood in three weeks at a cost of over £3000. Even the physical factors, therefore, of the Convention were conceived on a scale which gave some idea of the resources and convictions of the movement. The scene at the meeting was impressive to the last degree. The *Times* correspondent describes it as follows :—

The Scene at the Convention.

"On the same bench sat Conservatives and Liberals, Protestants and Roman Catholics. Throughout the whole Convention, which lasted about three hours, not one discordant note was heard; unanimity and enthusiasm reigned supreme; and when the Duke of Abercorn, with upraised arm, asserted, 'We will not have Home Rule,' the whole audience sprang to their feet and cheered for several minutes. There was no apathy about that demonstration nor about any which followed. Sir William Ewart moved the assemblage to another outburst when he stated that at the present time there were only four persons in Ireland in prison under any law but the ordinary law of the kingdom. Again, enthusiasm knew no bounds when Mr. Sinclair, a local merchant, having scouted the so-called justice of Catholic ascendency and shown its evils, said, 'Ulster makes no demands for Protestant ascendency, and we are determined, come what may, this hateful ascendency shall never be set over us.' But it was only when Mr. Andrews, in trumpet tones, asserted, 'As a last resource we will be prepared to defend ourselves,' that the feelings of the spectators appeared to lose all control, and found vent in cheers which lasted several minutes."

The City of Belfast was literally *en fête*. Bunting floated from every house. Tens of thousands arrived from all parts of Ulster, and the railway companies found it difficult, even with borrowed plant, to cope with the traffic. The demonstration was of such tremendous proportions that even the Gladstonian party were forced to admit its weight and significance.

The meeting opened, as it became the descendants of the Scot in Ulster and his English brethren, by acknowledging God in all His ways, with a portion of Scripture and with prayer and praise.* The effect of the immense assemblage singing the 46th Psalm, "God is our refuge and our strength," was thrilling and impressive to the last extent. The Duke of Abercorn, the lineal descendant of James Hamilton, who first planted County Down, occupied the chair.

---

* The Lord Primate of Ireland read the following prayer :—
"Almighty God, Father of our Lord Jesus Christ, who keepeth covenant and promise for ever, the life of those who flee to Thee, the hope of those who put their trust in Thee, mercifully regard the prayers of Thy servants now taking counsel in Thy name. Shed abroad upon us Thy Holy Spirit to guide our deliberations for the advancement of Thy glory, the safety of the Throne, and the integrity of the Empire. Give us firm resolve and power, and strength and fortitude to bring them to a successful issue, not, O God, in our own strength, but under Thy guidance, that we, being armed with Thy defence, may preserve, secure from all peril, our civil and religious liberty. Unite us together in the bonds of mutual love in the face of a common danger. Let truth and justice, brotherly kindness and charity, devotion and piety, dwell amongst us, that the course of this world and the prosperity of this country may be so peacefully ordered by Thy governance that we may joyfully serve Thee in all godly quietness, through Jesus Christ our Lord. Amen."

The speeches were strong and earnest, but on the whole moderate, and couched in the spirit of protest and appeal rather than of defiance. In them is contained the case of Ulster against Home Rule, and it is proposed to set that case forth here as nearly as may be in the very words of the speakers.

Composition of the Convention.

The significance of this great assembly, in all its circumstances without parallel in the history of Ireland, and probably in that of any other country, lay in its unique composition. The delegates who crowded the hall represented every rank, every class, and every Protestant creed in Ulster. Some came from the landlords of the province, some from the tenant-farmers, whose untiring industry had enriched the sterile soil of Ulster, some from the labourers by whom the fruits of the earth are gathered, and from the artisans. Amongst and behind them were the captains of industries; then came the toilers in the ranks of labour, who spend their lives at the ship, the engine, and the loom, whose hands wield the hammer, and whose skill directs the shuttle. Delegates were sent by the members of the Church that was once established; by the men who have held fast to the Presbyterian faith bequeathed to them by their Scottish ancestors; by the descendants of English Puritans who in their own land suffered for conscience' sake; by the sons of those who gave Wesley his earliest congregations, and

whose creed is still known by his honoured name.*
There were Roman Catholics, too, on the platform in
full acknowledgment by Protestant Ulster of their right
to all the privileges of British citizenship.†

All sections of politics were united on this meeting
—Conservatives, Liberals and Radicals. No Liberal
leader ever had in former days more devoted friends
and adherents than Mr. Gladstone possessed in the
north of Ireland, including all classes and creeds of
the community. Where are those followers now?
The answer lies in one significant fact. At the General
Elections of 1874 and 1880 the Liberal representation
of Ulster was considerably increased; so much so that
the party was emboldened to undertake the building
of the Ulster Reform Club in Belfast. The Club was
opened in 1885 at a cost of £20,000, and flourishes
now with a large membership. But the Liberal Club,
with the exception of a score of members at the most,
has renounced its allegiance to the chief for whom
they spent years of work and devotion, and there are
no stauncher Unionists to-day than the men who
organised it.

Behind this marvellous demonstration stood the
history of three centuries. The race that against all
odds made the bleak northern province what it is
to-day; the race that held it for the Empire, and in the
Revolution struggle of 1688; the race that so powerfully

* His Grace the Duke of Abercorn.
† Rev. R. R. Kane.

shared in founding and organising the great Republic of the west; the race that furnished the saviours of India in the dark days of the Mutiny ;—this race, in the Belfast Convention, declared that it must be satisfied in its sentiment, in its judgment, and in its conscience before it will consent to surrender or alter one jot or one tittle of the position of dignity and security which it now holds in the constitution and the fortunes of the Empire of the Queen.

Character of Ulstermen.

It does not follow that because the people of Ulster are not always agitating and attending political meetings and desecrating the Sabbath they are not an *earnest people*. They are very earnest in their habits; but, above all, they are an *industrious* people, and strangers have only to visit the north of Ireland and the great centres of commercial activity to witness proofs of their industry. *Industry is their first object*, not agitation. But if agitation is necessary to protect their industries, then it will be found that that protection is forthcoming; and with protection comes action.

Ulstermen have been described by hostile critics as a spoilt and pampered race, arrogantly claiming privileges beyond their countrymen. They have been derided as cowards. Their protests have been sneered at as empty bluster. The reply to these taunts is to be found in their past history and the present position of their province. Before Ulster was planted by Scotch and English settlers it was the poorest and most turbulent part of Ireland. It consisted for the most part of waste and forest, where lawless chiefs attempting to govern yet more lawless subjects lived in constant strife. Was it cowardice and bluster that enabled the Protestant settlers, during the first century of their existence there, to hold their own amidst a hostile population with no other aid than that of their own strong arms? Were these their weapons in the dark and evil days towards its close, when, almost forsaken by the mother-country, they upheld the cause of faith and freedom? But there is a better test than siege or battle. Let the Ulstermen be judged by the noble victories of peace. Their energy has given richness and fertility to a sterile soil. Their towns are alive with many industries. Their ports send vessels laden with manufactures to every land. Their shipbuilders are adding yearly to the commercial navies of the world. These are things that can only be achieved by a strong and self-reliant people; and such are the men who proclaimed to the world in the Belfast Convention, that their prosperity and liberties must not be jeopardised by the rash experiments of party politicians.*

Motive of the Meeting.

A conviction of common duty in the presence of a

* Duke of Abercorn.

common danger having healed divisions that formerly embittered many social relationships in Ulster, the mainspring and motive force of the Convention was declared to be a united defence by Ulstermen of their common birthright as British citizens. Their position was that the establishment of a Parliament in Dublin will only destroy the peace and security enjoyed under Imperial rule in Ireland, and do a grievous wrong to the people whose only offence is their loyalty to Great Britain and their pride in sharing her greatness. They hold that in one kingdom there should be only one Parliament, and one set of lawmakers for the whole of the United Kingdom (just as in one body there should be only one head); so that the people of Cork and the people of Middlesex, and the people of Kerry and the people of Midlothian, shall all in common be subject to the laws made for them in the pure and clear atmosphere of the great democratic Parliament of Great Britain and Ireland. The object of the Ulster Convention was neither to prop up an unjust ascendency nor to utter a shout of bigotry, but in the name of a million and a half of free men, born in the fulness of the freedom of the British Constitution, to put on record before the world their solemn determination to continue free, and to put on record also their solemn appeal to the British people and to civilised mankind whether they are not justified in this determination. The North does not ask to govern the South. Both have lived under the same laws. The South have been indolent, thriftless, and complaining. The North has been industrious, self-reliant and prosperous. The men who manned the Convention hold that there is but one thing under the sun that can give them security—security for their civil and religious rights, for their land interests, for their commercial, manufacturing and educational interests, and that is the broad ægis of the British Constitution. Under that they can get a clear riddance of any existing grievances, while Home Rule would only be an exchange of troubles.

Justification of the Union.

Since the Union Ulster has advanced with steady pace in a degree not surpassed by any other portion of the United Kingdom, and she demands that she shall remain fully represented in the Imperial Parliament, to whose protection she owes her welfare. Why should she be driven from it? Ulster loyal members have never obstructed, have never wasted time, but have given faithful and intelligent service in promoting useful legislation for the whole kingdom, and under the protection of that Parliament capital has been invested and industries established and fostered. The mere shadow of the Home Rule Bill of 1886 lowered the value of bank and railway stocks in Ireland by seven million pounds, and all industries would be similarly affected. Mr. Gladstone may say that this would all recover, and that capital would again flow in as it has done in the past; but how could it recover if Ireland were in a state of continued turbulence, or if it were known to the world that Ulster was only kept from reasserting its loyalty by all the force that England and Scotland could use? The maintenance of Ulster's industries and the employment of her people depend upon her general and mercantile credit being maintained at its present high standard. They depend upon accumulated capital being safe from attack, on outside capital continuing to flow in for investment, and on freedom from excessive local taxation, which would assuredly be the only resort of a lavish and unpractical Government. Ulstermen have gained their position by simple means that are within reach of all, by no favours of climate or richness of soil, by no favouritism or special help from any Government, but by commonplace industry and perseverance, by honourable dealing and observance of contracts, by filling up all their time so that there is no place left for that sure offspring of idleness —the agitator and preacher of discontent and sedition.*

Has the Imperial Parliament shown incompetency to deal justly with Ireland? Let us see. The Irish Church has been disestablished and disendowed, so that there is no religious grievance. The land laws have advanced so far that no country in the world has better. There is a Land Commission to fix the rent of every agricultural holding, from a yearly tenancy to

* Sir W. K. Ewart.

the leaseholder whose lease expires within ninety-nine years of the passing of the Land Act of 1881. The Redemption of Rent Act provides that perpetuity and other leaseholders can demand from their landlords a sale of their farms at a price to be settled by the Land Commission. In case the landlord refuses to sell, the tenant can take him to the Land Court and have a fair rent fixed. By the Land Purchase Acts about forty-five millions of money have been placed at the disposal of the Commission to enable tenants to become owners of their farms on easy terms. A review of the last six years' British legislation shows no Irish grievance with which the Imperial Parliament is not capable of grappling.*

Not long since, when the late Government proposed to cede Heligoland to Germany, the Gladstonian leaders propounded the doctrine that the inhabitants of that island ought to be consulted as to whether they were willing to relinquish their allegiance to England. Why is the same doctrine not to be applied to the men of Ulster? Is it to be said that there was greater peril to the inhabitants of Heligoland in being handed over to the government of a great country, such as Germany, than to Ulstermen, whom it is proposed to hand over to be ruled by men who have been the promoters of the Land League and the Plan of Campaign? †

* Mr. Doloughan.
† Mr. Dunville.

Why and How Ulster will Fight.

The granting of Home Rule will bring to those who think they are asking for bread, not merely a stone, but a sword. The Protestants of the North of Ireland are children of the Revolution of 1688, and, cost what it may, they will have nothing to do with a Dublin Parliament. The Parliament of England has a right to govern Ulster, but no right to sell her into slavery.

What are the two forces that would be supreme in any possible Irish Parliament that could be called together? They are the forces represented by the Plan of Campaign on the one hand, and by Archbishop Walsh and the Irish priesthood on the other. The Plan of Campaign has been responsible for all the horrors and outrages which shocked the civilised world in the early years of the last Parliament, but which, owing to the wise, firm, and judicious rule of the late Government, have been stamped out and put an end to. Its authors and leaders have been branded by a high legal tribunal as men who have incited to intimidation when they knew that intimidation led to murder and outrage.* It did not matter whether it was a Protestant or Roman Catholic who crossed the will of the Home Rule *Vehmgericht*; he was a marked man, and mercy interposed in vain. It was not enough to

---

* Lord Erne.

slay the living; the vengeance of boycotter pursued the dead and robbed them of decent burial; and these things and worse were the direct results of the system set in force and approved by the men into whose hands Mr. Gladstone would fling Ulstermen to deal with them by their own police, their own judges, their own laws, and their own Parliament, a Parliament at the beck of Archbishop Walsh and his subservient hierarchy.* To such a Parliament, if it ever be even set up, Ulster will never elect members, will never acknowledge allegiance, and its right to tax will be utterly repudiated. Its existence will simply be ignored. Its Acts will be but as waste paper; its police will find the barracks of Ulster preoccupied with her own constabulary; its judges will sit in empty court-houses. The early efforts of its executive will be spent in devising means to deal with a passive resistance to its taxation co-extensive with loyalist Ulster. Those who desire the luxury of Home Rule will be allowed to enjoy its legislation and pay for it themselves. Their kinsmen of the American Revolution have taught Ulstermen to leave it to those that will force tyranny and injustice upon them to strike the first blow. If England and Scotland are determined to force Ulster into civil war, on them let the responsibility rest. As a last extremity her sons will be prepared to defend themselves, and they will not be without allies.†

* Rev. Dr. Lynd.
† Mr. Thomas Sinclair and Mr. Thomas Andrews.

The Resolution Arrived at by the Belfast Convention.

There only remains to give the terms of the resolution arrived at by the mind and will of the Ulster Loyalists. They need no further comment, and are in themselves an appeal and a warning to the men who are endeavouring to break up the United Kingdom. They run as follows:—

"That this Convention, consisting of 11,879 delegates representing the Unionists of every creed, class, and party throughout Ulster appointed at public meetings held in every electoral division of the province, hereby resolves and declares:—

" 1. That we express the devoted loyalty of Ulster Unionists to the Crown and Constitution of the United Kingdom.

" 2. That we avow our fixed resolve to retain unchanged our present position as an integral portion of the United Kingdom, and to protest in the most unequivocal manner against the passage of any measure that would rob us of our inheritance in the Imperial Parliament, under the protection of which our capital has been invested, and our homes and rights safeguarded.

" 3. That we record our determination to have nothing to do with a Parliament certain to be controlled by men responsible for the crime and outrage of the Land League, the dishonesty of the Plan of Campaign, and the cruelties of boycotting, many of whom have shown themselves the ready instruments of clerical domination.

"4. That we declare to the people of Great Britain our conviction that the attempt to set up such a Parliament in Ireland will inevitably result in disorder, violence, and bloodshed, such as have not been experienced in this century, and to announce our resolve to take no part in the election or the proceedings of such a Parliament, the authority of which, should it ever be constituted, we shall be forced to repudiate.

"5. That we protest against this great question, which involves our lives, property, and civil rights, being treated as a mere side-issue in the impending electoral struggle.

"6. That we appeal to those of our fellow-countrymen who have hitherto been in favour of a separate Parliament to abandon a demand which hopelessly divides Irishmen, and to unite with us under the Imperial Legislature in developing the resources and furthering the best interests of our common country.

"7. That we, the Unionists of Ulster, desire to offer to our brother Unionists inhabiting the other provinces of Ireland the assurance of our profound sympathy, to place on record our conviction that their interests and their perils are identical with our own, and to declare our fixed resolve to make common cause with them in resisting the attempt to impose a Home Rule Parliament upon our country."

CHAPTER XVIII.

CONCLUSION.

LET us now take a broad view of the facts disclosed during the past ten years in Ireland in these pages, and endeavour to summarise a conclusion as to the chances of civil and religious liberty under an Irish Government elected under pressure of the Roman Catholic Hierarchy and priesthood.

These facts, it is submitted, have been fully established:

1. The existence of an organised clerical conspiracy in Ireland to resist the law, abet agrarian conspiracies, and foment political disturbances amongst the people.

2. The putting forward of mediæval claims on the part of the Roman Catholic Hierarchy and priesthood that the political views they may at any particular time entertain shall be free from public criticism.

3. The frank expression of further claims of the priesthood to be exempt from civil jurisdiction, to dispense with, to supersede, and to overrule the law of the land and every other law or moral obligation when clashing with the interests of clericalism.

4. The further claim of the Roman Catholic Hier-

archy to make every political question one of morals, to make it a mortal sin to vote against the wishes of the priesthood, and to make the Court of Rome the ultimate court of appeal in all Irish questions.

5. The existence in Ireland amongst a certain section of the population and their leaders of views and intentions to replace an extinct Protestant ascendency by a new Roman Catholic ascendency, and to use all the resources of a Home Rule Government for this purpose.

6. The absolute power, in three out of four provinces of Ireland, of the Irish priest in all movements political and social, with ample proof that he is willing and able to wield it in any particular way, with or without the permission of his superiors.

7. Demonstration of the fact that it is possible for the politics of Ireland to be almost completely controlled for a set purpose by thirty prelates who have been placed by the Pope of Rome in command of the civil and religious opinions of the Roman Catholic community in that country.

These facts in themselves show clearly the enormous influence of the dominant religion in Roman Catholic Ireland. In the opinion of the heads of that Church, Roman Catholicism is nothing if it is not everything. *Aut Cæsar aut nullus.* In the Middle Ages the Papacy in its struggle with the Empire failed to obtain the recognition of its universal sovereignty. To-day, in a Catholic country like Ireland, she has every opportunity of doing so in a very simple and effective manner.

Let the clergy use the pulpit and confessional, as was done in Meath and half the constituencies of Ireland at the general election of 1892; let them nominate members of Parliament and carry them to the head of the poll, *vi et armis*, and the thing is done. The triumph of Ultramontanism is complete. It has broken down all the barriers which ought to restrain ecclesiastical action and mark the boundaries of civil and religious spheres; it becomes superior to the State. The people are not allowed to appeal to their own judgment and reason in political matters; they are not even allowed to examine the grounds of the Church's assumed authority. Under such conditions, with Home Rule, the Pope will be sovereign in Ireland, and the Cardinal-elect will be his Viceroy.

For years the Nationalist party have posed as the representatives of a people "rightly struggling to be free." But to real civil and religious freedom they must be utterly indifferent. The facts placed here in detail prove this to demonstration. If it be not the object, the logical result of the victory of the majority of the Irish Nationalist party must be, not to free the people, but to enslave them. The foot of the priest will be planted still more firmly on the neck of his flock, the foot of the bishop still more firmly on the neck of the priest, and the foot of the Pope still more firmly on the neck of the bishop. Everything that gives strength and dignity to human nature will be sacrificed to Ultramontanism.

CONCLUSION. 211

So long as the Imperial Parliament exists such a state of things is impossible. The counteracting force of such a mixed assembly is supreme. The erection of a Roman Catholic Parliament in Dublin is in itself the contradiction in terms of the ideal of democratic government, and can lead to nothing but weltering confusion and inevitable bloodshed. But it may be said that Mr. Redmond's independent party in Ireland may be looked upon as a possible lever against priestly intolerance. The results of the fresh Meath elections do not tend to strengthen this theory. Indeed, what chance have such a party against the tremendous forces arrayed against them? They must always occupy a contradictory position. It has been said, and will be said again, independent Catholics who are really Catholics are not independent, and those who are really independent are not Catholic; in other words, under Home Rule independent Catholicism will be a contradiction in terms. Placed in such a dilemma they must always be exposed to a tremendous crossfire of attack, which may be resisted by a small body of leaders, but which the rank and file of rural Irishmen are not likely long to survive. What chance, in the face of such difficulties, is there for a resurgence of the spirit of civil liberty in three out of four provinces of Ireland? The chance is indeed remote. Under Home Rule the difficulties of preserving civil liberty in Ireland will become tremendous. In some Roman Catholic countries no doubt we see very free democratic institutions ruling quietly and peaceably. In the Tyrol, for example, and in a portion of Canada, the people obey the priest, or rather they partake of the priest's ideas and sentiments in everything. But this is not freedom. It is despotism veiled under a veneer of democracy. The religious sentiment is indispensable for the proper exercise of liberty in its widest sense. But when religion becomes a political instrument in the hands of a clerical party whose object it is to enthrone the priest, and exempt him from civil jurisdiction, then society must inevitably be rent and torn asunder with the violence of the struggles which will ensue. This is the warning which Ulster desires to give Great Britain, not in a spirit of sectarianism and bigotry, but with the object of laying bare the bed-rock of modern Irish history, and all the social, political, and religious differences which have been reared upon it.

THE END.

Printed by Hazell, Watson, & Viney, Ld., London and Aylesbury.

www.ingramcontent.com/pod-product-compliance
Lightning Source LLC
Chambersburg PA
CBHW031818230426
43669CB00009B/1183